629.2844

THE
CERTIFICATE OF
PROFESSIONAL
COMPETENCE

D0303322

THE
CERTIFICATE OF PROFESSIONAL COMPETENCE

Revised third edition

1001 TYPICAL QUESTIONS AND ANSWERS FOR THE ROAD GOODS NATIONAL AND INTERNATIONAL EXAMINATIONS

DAVID LOWE

The Chartered Institute of
Logistics and Transport (UK)

KOGAN
PAGE

Limerick Institute of Technology · LIBRARY
Institiúid Teicneolaíochta Luimnigh · LEABHARLANN
Class No. 629·2844 LOW
Acc. No. 30335
Date: 4 March 2009

Publisher's note

Every possible effort has been made to ensure that the information contained in this book is accurate at the time of going to press, and the publisher and author cannot accept reponsibility for any errors or omissions, however caused. No responsibility for loss or damage occasioned to any person acting, or refraining from action, as a result of the material in this publication can be accepted by the publisher or the author.

First published in 1990
Second edition 1995
Third edition 2001
Revised third edition 2005
Reprinted in 2006, 2008

Apart from any fair dealing for the purposes of research or private study, or criticism or review, as permitted under the Copyright, Designs and Patents Act 1988, this publication may only be reproduced, stored or transmitted, in any form or by any means, with the prior permission in writing of the publishers, or in the case of reprographic reproduction in accordance with the terms and licences issued by the CLA. Enquiries concerning reproduction outside these terms should be sent to the publishers at the undermentioned address:

Kogan Page Limited
120 Pentonville Road
London N1 9JN

© David Lowe, 1990, 1995, 2001, 2005

The right of David Lowe to be identified as the author of this work has been asserted by him in accordance with the Copyright, Designs and Patents Act 1988.

British Library Cataloguing in Publication Data

A CIP record for this book is available from the British Library.

ISBN 978 0 7494 4338 2

Typeset by Saxon Graphics Ltd, Derby
Printed and bound in Great Britain by Biddles Ltd, King's Lynn, Norfolk

Contents

Acknowledgements

I am grateful for permission to use a number of questions originally published by the former Royal Society of Arts in its typical examination papers. I also acknowledge the permission given by Oxford Cambridge and RSA Examinations (or OCR) to reproduce a number of its typical case-study scenarios and answers and for the use of the examination syllabus reproduced in this book.

Acknowledgements

Introduction

The legal requirement for professional competence was introduced in the UK (at the instigation of the European Community, as the EU was then called) on 1 January 1978 as a condition under which a standard operator's licence would be granted to permit the carriage of goods for hire or reward in either purely national or both national and international transport operations. Provisions in the regulations originally enabled certain people engaged in the road transport industry at that time to claim their 'professional competence' on the grounds of qualifying experience by obtaining a 'Grandfather Rights' Certificate of Professional Competence (CPC). Individuals who did not qualify under this scheme (which ended on 31 December 1979) may satisfy the requirements by holding membership, at specified grades, of one of the professional transport institutes. For those who do not qualify by these methods, however, and for new entrants to the industry in future years, an examination system has been established which provides the professional competence qualification.

The collection of typical CPC questions in this book is intended to help those people taking the official examinations who need or want to acquire the professional competence qualification in order to take up positions in transport. Its purpose is to provide readers with a means of revision and self-testing of the knowledge required for the national and international examinations in road haulage and to familiarize themselves with the various types of question set in the examinations. It should help candidates to study privately, at home and elsewhere, when just a few spare moments are available for revision or when it is convenient to devote longer periods to study.

The multiple-choice questions included are typical of the type used in the examinations, a number of them having actually been used in past examinations. The last part of this book comprises a new type of question used since October 1999, when revised examination requirements demanded by the EU came into being. These are based on given case-study scenarios, which the examinee must read carefully and then show an understanding of the situation portrayed by setting out a clear and concise answer. There are no clues with these questions, unlike the multiple-choice questions, where a guess may prove to be lucky. Answers for all the questions are provided at the end of the book.

To help potential examinees, the text also includes information on the legal requirements for professional competence and on the examination system, as well as giving details of the current official OCR (Oxford Cambridge and RSA Examinations) syllabus. Readers will see that the syllabus covers a broad range of subjects – from matters directly concerning the legal and administrative aspects of goods vehicle operation to technical aspects of vehicle construction and use, maintenance and road safety measures. It also covers the much wider issues of business management such as administration, financial control, knowledge of the law and the structure of business, plus the complexities of social legislation. The typical questions included in the book reflect this broad range of subjects.

This revised third edition of the book follows the sequence of the current OCR syllabus (effective since October 1999) and has been updated to include changes in the law up to July 2004.

CHAPTER 1

Requirement for professional competence

The Goods Vehicles (Licensing of Operators) Act 1995, as amended by SI 1999/2430 and European Council Directive 96/26/EC amended by Directive 98/76/EC, requires that individuals or transport firms that wish to engage in the carriage of goods by road for hire or reward and consequently, in the UK, need to hold a standard operator's licence, must satisfy conditions of professional competence either by the operator personally holding the qualification or by the employment of a person who is professionally competent. A person in this position who did not qualify under the original 'Grandfather Rights' provisions mentioned earlier, or who is not exempt on the basis of institute membership, must pass the official OCR examination (based on the syllabus contained in Annex I to the EC Directive mentioned above) in order to qualify for professional competence.

Note: Copies of the above-mentioned Act and Statutory Instruments and of the EC Directives may be obtained from The Stationery Office (formerly HMSO) or from local booksellers that stock official publications.

VALIDATION WITHIN THE EU

Those individuals who qualify for professional competence in Great Britain and who wish either to operate a road haulage business or to obtain a position as a transport manager in a haulage business based outside Great Britain, whether in Northern Ireland or in any other member state of the European Union* (since in either capacity for any such territory they will need to show they are professionally competent), can obtain a 'Certificate of Qualification' confirming this by applying to a Traffic Commissioner and paying the appropriate fee (currently £20).

*Note: Austria, Belgium, Cyprus, Czech Republic, Denmark, Estonia, Finland, France, Germany, Greece, Hungary, the Irish Republic, Italy, Latvia, Lithuania, Luxembourg, Malta, the Netherlands, Poland, Portugal, Slovakia, Slovenia, Spain and Sweden were the other member states of the European Union in July 2004 – the EU was enlarged to 25 member states in May 2004.

CHAPTER 2

The OCR syllabus

A study syllabus covering the professional competence examination in road haulage is available from the Oxford Cambridge and RSA (OCR) Board (see below for address). Study may be undertaken at courses, which are run by a number of bodies including trade associations and commercial organizations. Some local technical colleges and other teaching establishments also offer part-time (usually evening) classes on the subject.

The study may involve full-time or part-time attendance at such courses or it may be by correspondence course, with a home-learning package (eg notes and cassette tapes) or with the aid of teaching manuals. The author's *A Study Manual of Professional Competence in Road Haulage* (11th edition, published by Kogan Page, London) has been used successfully by many examination candidates without resorting to attendance at study courses or evening classes.

Examination candidates should note that examination questions will be based on the syllabus as published. Where current legislation is changed, the content will not be examined for at least three months from the date of implementation. Where current legislation remains unchanged in detail, yet becomes embodied within new legislation, the content will continue to be examined. Legislation that has been repealed or revoked will not be examined.

Those wishing to study for the examination should ensure that they have an up-to-date syllabus, available from the Oxford Cambridge and RSA Information Bureau (OCR), Progress House, Westwood Way, Coventry CV4 8JQ (tel: 02476 470033; fax: 02476 421944; website:

www.ocr.org.uk. Examinations are held four times a year at approved centres; contact OCR for details of dates and places.

THE CPC SYLLABUS

The syllabus for national and international road haulage operations (effective from 1 October 1999) is reproduced here.

A. Civil Law   *Relevant modules: 1, 2, 4 & 6*

Assessment objectives mean that candidates must:

A1.
Be familiar with the main types of contract used in road transport and with the rights and obligations arising therefrom.

> **Topics covered**
> - contracts;
> - legal obligations;
> - subcontracting;
> - legal duties of agents, employers and employees.

A2.
Be capable of negotiating a legally valid transport contract, notably with regard to conditions of carriage.

> **Topics covered**
> - legal obligations;
> - capacity to contract;
> - specific performance;
> - liability;
> - lien;
> - laws of agency.

A3.
Be able to consider a claim by their principal regarding compensation for loss of or damage to goods during transportation or for their late delivery, and to understand how such claims affect their contractual responsibility.

> **Topics covered**
> - performance – general and specific liabilities of principal, subcontractors and agents for the performance of a contract;
> - compensation – for losses relating to damage;
> - settlements – interim and full payments.

A4.
Be familiar with the rules and obligations arising from the CMR Convention on the contract for the international carriage of goods by road.

> **Topics covered**
> - CMR liability and unwitting CMR;
> - CMR notes to CMR convention;
> - successive carriers;
> - limits of liability;
> - relevance of insurance.

B. Commercial Law   *Relevant modules: 1 & 4*

Assessment objectives mean that candidates must:

B1.
Be familiar with the conditions and formalities laid down for plying the trade, the general obligations incumbent upon transport operators (eg registration, keeping records) and the consequences of bankruptcy.

> **Topics covered**
>
> Trading law relating to:
> - sole traders and partnerships;
> - partnership agreements;
> - rights and duties of partners;
> - powers of partners;
> - partners as agents;
> - dissolution of partnerships.
>
> Company law:
> - registered companies (private and public);
> - AGMs;
> - liquidation.
>
> Documentation:
> - Prospectus;
> - Memorandum of Association;
> - Articles of Association;
> - Certificate of Incorporation.

B2.

Have appropriate knowledge of the various forms of commercial company and the rules governing their constitution.

Topics covered

Types of business organization:
- sole traders;
- partnerships;
- private and public limited companies;
- co-operatives.

C. Social Law   *Relevant modules: 1, 4 & 6*

Assessment objectives mean that candidates must:

C1.

Be familiar with the role and function of the various social institutions which are concerned with road transport (trade unions, works councils, shop stewards, labour inspectors).

Topics covered

Role of:
- employment tribunals;
- trade unions;
- ACAS;
- arbitrators;
- DTI.

Employees' rights:
- trade union membership;
- trade union activities.

C2.

Be familiar with the employers' social security obligations.

Topics covered

Relevant parts of current legislation relating to:
- health and safety;
- discrimination;
- employment protection;
- employment rights.

C3.
Be familiar with the rules governing work contracts for the various categories of worker employed by road transport undertakings (form of the contracts, obligations of the parties, working conditions and working hours, paid leave, remuneration, breach of contract).

Topics covered

Contracts of employment:
- content of written statement;
- time limits for the issue of contracts.

Employment rights:
- full- and part-time employees;
- self-employed;
- agency staff;
- transfer of undertakings;
- remuneration and itemized pay statements;
- holiday entitlement;
- dismissal and unfair dismissal;
- notice to terminate employment;
- working-time regulations.

C4.
Be familiar with the provisions on driving periods and rest periods laid down in Regulation (EEC) 3820/85, the provisions of Regulation (EEC) 3821/85 on recording equipment in road transport and the practical arrangements for implementing these regulations.

Topics covered

Community regulations:
- the working week;
- driving time;
- breaks;
- daily and weekly rest periods;
- emergencies.

Domestic hours' law:
- the working week;
- driving time;
- rest periods;
- emergencies.

Tachograph legislation and operation:
- points of law;
- the records;
- driver and employer responsibilities;
- enforcement and inspection;
- calibration and sealing;
- malfunctions.

D. Fiscal Law   *Relevant modules: 1, 2, 4 & 6*

Assessment objectives mean that candidates must:

D1.
Be familiar with the rules governing VAT on transport services.

Topics covered

VAT – national operations:
- income threshold and registration;
- zero-rated goods and services;
- VAT returns;
- reclaiming VAT.

Turnover tax – international operations:
- registration for VAT;
- applying VAT;
- submitting returns;
- reclaiming VAT.

D2.
Be familiar with motor vehicle tax.

Topics covered

Calculation of VED:
- basis for calculating motor vehicle taxation on general vehicles;
- basis for calculation on vehicles used in special operations;
- conditions applied to vehicles taxed for use in special operations.

D3.
Be familiar with taxes on certain road haulage vehicles and tolls and infra-structure user charges.

Topics covered
- domestic operation – toll roads and bridges;
- domestic operation – the basis on which tolls are calculated;
- international operation – rules governing tolls and taxation of vehicles on international journeys.

D4.
Be familiar with the relevant regulations on income tax.

Topics covered

- corporate taxation;
- double taxation;
- status – rules governing the status of employees and the self-employed and the imposition of income tax regulations;
- employers' responsibilities – deduction and collection of income tax and National Insurance from employees;
- employers' responsibility for payment of income tax and National Insurance to Inland Revenue).

E. Business and financial management of the undertaking
Relevant modules: 1, 2, 4 & 6

Assessment objectives mean that candidates must:

E1.
Be familiar with the laws and practices regarding the use of cheques, bills of exchange, promissory notes, credit cards and other means or methods of payment.

Topics covered

National operation – payment methods:
- cash;
- cheques;
- credit cards;
- promissory notes;
- bills of exchange;
- debit systems and credit transfer.

International operation:
- banking and payment systems;
- electronic transfer of funds (eg Swift, Eurocheques).

E2.
Be familiar with the various forms of credit (bank credit, documentary credit, guarantee deposits, mortgages, leasing, renting, factoring) and with the charges and obligations arising from them.

> **Topics covered**
>
> Different forms of credit:
> - overdrafts;
> - loans;
> - documentary credit;
> - guarantee deposits;
> - mortgages;
> - leases;
> - rents;
> - factoring.

E3.

Know what a balance sheet is, how it is set out and how to interpret it.

> **Topics covered**
>
> Determine:
> - fixed assets;
> - net current assets;
> - current assets;
> - long-term liabilities;
> - current liabilities;
> - interpretation of figures for assets and liabilities.

E4.

Be able to read and interpret a profit-and-loss account.

> **Topics covered**
>
> Determine:
> - direct and indirect costs;
> - gross (or operating or trading) profit;
> - net profit.

E5.

Be able to assess the company's profitability and financial position, in particular on the basis of financial ratios.

> **Topics covered**
>
> Determine:
> - capital employed and return on capital employed;
> - return on sales and assets turnover;
> - working capital;
> - cash flow.
>
> Use of ratios:
> - current ratio (working capital ratio);
> - quick ratio (liquidity ratio or acid test ratio).

E6.
Be able to prepare a budget.

> **Topics covered**
>
> Construct budgets from data supplied:
> - use to monitor and control performance;
> - use of budgetary control;
> - use of variance analysis.

E7.
Be familiar with their company's cost elements (fixed costs, variable costs, working capital, depreciation, etc), and be able to calculate costs per vehicle, per kilometre, per journey and per tonne.

> **Topics covered**
>
> From data supplied, identify and/or calculate:
> - fixed costs;
> - variable costs;
> - overhead costs;
> - depreciation;
> - time and distance costs.

E8.
Be able to draw up an organization chart relating to the undertaking's personnel as a whole and to organize work plans.

> **Topics covered**
>
> Prepare an organization chart (organizing, planning and measuring work) for an:
> - organization;
> - department;
> - function;
> - unit; or
> - depot.

E9.

Be familiar with the principles of marketing, publicity and public relations, including transport services, sales promotion and the preparation of customer files.

Topics covered

Marketing:
- market research (primary and secondary);
- segmentation;
- product promotion and sales and publicity;
- customer relations;
- customer-research files.

E10.

Be familiar with the different types of insurance relating to road transport (liability, accidental injury/life insurance) and with the guarantees and obligations arising therefrom.

Topics covered

Insurance:
- risk assessment;
- cover;
- claims;
- risk management;
- improvement of risk.

Types of insurance:
- fidelity;
- goods-in-transit;
- employers' liability;
- public liability;
- professional negligence;
- motor;
- plant;
- travel;
- health;
- property;
- consequential loss;
- cash-in-transit.

Risks:
- guarantees;
- obligations;
- liability and role of trustees.

E11.

Be familiar with the applications of electronic data transmission in road transport.

> **Topics covered**
>
> Legislation – Data Protection Act. Hardware and software:
> - electronic vehicle-status monitoring;
> - electronic data transmission;
> - real-time information systems;
> - customer information systems;
> - depot readers;
> - GPS;
> - route and load planning systems;
> - vehicle and staff scheduling;
> - data analysis;
> - data information systems.

E12.

Be able to apply the rules governing the invoicing of road haulage services and know the meaning of Incoterms.

> **Topics covered**
>
> Transactions and the purpose of:
> - quotations;
> - orders;
> - consignment notes;
> - Incoterms and their principal provisions applying to any mode of road transport, including multimodal.

Note: Incoterms are agreed trading terms with legal definitions, eg FOB. The International Chamber of Commerce produces a book called *Incoterms* (Ref: ISBN 92-842-0087-3).

E13.

Be familiar with the different categories of transport auxiliaries, their role, their functions and, where appropriate, their status.

> **Topics covered**
>
> Agents who assist in ensuring freight is properly and correctly transferred, for example:
> - freight forwarders;
> - shippers;
> - clearing houses;
> - groupage operators.

F. Access to the market   *Relevant modules: 2, 4 & 6*

Assessment objectives mean that candidates must:

F1.

Be familiar with the occupational regulations governing road transport for hire or reward, industrial vehicle rental and subcontracting, and in particular the rules governing the official organization of the occupation, admission to the occupation, authorizations for intra- and extra-Community road transport operations, inspections and sanctions.

Topics covered

National operation:
- role of Traffic Commissioners and enforcement agencies;
- statutory procedures concerning operator licensing;
- requirements for vehicle maintenance;
- regulations governing domestic operation.

International operation:
- statutory procedures concerning operator licensing;
- regulations governing international operations.

F2.

Be familiar with the rules for setting up a road transport undertaking.

Topics covered

- rules for setting up a road transport undertaking;
- statutory procedures;
- rules concerning operator licensing.

F3.

Be familiar with the various documents required for operating road transport services and be able to introduce checking procedures for ensuring that the approved documents relating to each transport operation, and in particular those relating to the vehicle, the driver and the goods or luggage, are kept both in the vehicle and on the premises of the undertaking.

Topics covered

Documents and their administration:
- operator licences and vehicle discs;
- vehicle authorizations;
- tachograph records;
- waybills/consignment notes;
- driving entitlement;
- maintenance documents;
- insurance documents;
- systems for document checking and
- control procedures.

F4.

Be familiar with the rules on the organization of the market in road haulage services, on freight handling and logistics.

Topics covered

- market organization:
  - 1985 Transport Act,
  - regulatory powers of the Secretary of State,
  - regulatory powers of the Office of Fair Trading,
  - the Monopolies and Mergers Commission;
- role of local government regarding the movement of abnormal loads;
- main provisions of third-country traffic and cabotage.

F5.

Be familiar with frontier formalities, the role and scope of 'T' documents and TIR carnets, and the obligations and responsibilities arising from their use.

Topics covered

- 'T' documents, their status and rules of use;
- carnets, and rules governing their use;
- practical use of various exemptions obtained by the use of various documents and the implications for operators and their customers.

G. Technical standards and aspects of operation
Relevant modules: 2, 4 & 6

Assessment objectives mean that candidates must:

G1.

Be familiar with the rules concerning the weights and dimensions of vehicles in the member states of the European Union and the procedures to be followed in the case of abnormal loads which constitute an exception to these rules.

Topics covered

- terms used to identify the differing weight conditions;
- statutory limits – weights and dimensions;
- formulas used for various calculations concerned in weights and dimensions of vehicles;
- main rules and most common weights and dimensions used internationally.

G2.

Be able to choose vehicles and their components (chassis, engine, transmission system, braking system, etc) in accordance with the needs of the undertaking.

Topics covered
- vehicle specifications that will improve road safety;
- vehicle specifications to increase economy and reduce impact on the environment;
- vehicle specifications for international operations.

G3.

Be familiar with the formalities relating to the type approval, registration and technical inspection of these vehicles.

Topics covered
- main provisions within current legislation relating to C&U and safety;
- powers of enforcement agencies.

G4.

Understand what measures must be taken to reduce noise and to combat air pollution by motor vehicle exhaust emissions.

Topics covered
- main provisions of the C&U regulations;
- EU Directives and environmental legislation;
- training, including awareness training.

G5.

Be able to draw up periodic maintenance plans for the vehicles and their equipment.

Topics covered

Maintenance programmes:
- planned preventive;
- methods of maintenance;
- operator's obligations and liabilities to maintain vehicles and equipment in a safe, roadworthy condition;
- responsibility for vehicles whose maintenance is contracted out.

G6.

Be familiar with the different types of cargo-handling and loading devices (tailboards, containers, pallets, etc) and be able to introduce procedures and issue instructions for loading and unloading goods (load distribution, stacking, stowing, blocking and chocking).

Topics covered
- risk analysis and safe operations;
- requirements for various loads and
- procedures to ensure safe operations.

G7.

Be familiar with the various techniques of 'piggy-back' and roll-on/roll-off combined transport.

Topics covered
- safety requirements;
- vehicle specifications;
- charging methods.

G8.

Be able to implement procedures for complying with the rules on the carriage of dangerous goods and waste, notably those arising from:

- Directive 94/55/EC on the approximation of the laws of the member states with regard to the transport of dangerous goods by road;
- Directive 96/35/EC on the appointment and vocational qualification of safety advisers for the transport of dangerous goods by road, rail and inland waterway;
- Regulation (EEC) 259/93 on the supervision and control of shipments of waste within, into and out of the European Community.

Topics covered

Ensure main provisions of regulations are identified and incorporated into a procedure to meet current requirements:
- national;
- international.

G9.

Be able to implement procedures for complying with the rules on the carriage of perishable foodstuffs, notably those arising from the agreement on the international carriage of perishable foodstuffs and on the special equipment to be used for such carriage (ATP).

> **Topics covered**
>
> Procedures to ensure:
> - correct compliance with legislation;
> - best practice.

G10.

Be able to implement procedures for complying with the rules on the transport of live animals.

> **Topics covered**
>
> National and international procedures to ensure:
> - correct compliance with legislation;
> - best practice.

H. Road safety   *Relevant modules: 2, 4 & 6*

Assessment objectives mean that candidates must:

H1.

Know what qualifications are required for drivers – driving licences, medical certificates, certificates of fitness.

> **Topics covered**
>
> - vocational entitlements – different categories, types and qualifications for driving licences and entitlements;
> - procedures relating to the issue, renewal, revocation and production of licences and removal of entitlements;
> - disciplinary matters – procedures and appeals;
> - Driving tests scope and conduct, and sequence of theory and driving tests;
> - International driving permits, their issue and validation.

H2.

Be able to take the necessary steps to ensure that drivers comply with the traffic rules, prohibitions and restrictions in force in the different Member States of the European Union relating to speed limits, priorities, waiting and parking restrictions, use of lights, road signs.

Topics covered

Traffic regulations:
- signs and signals;
- variation in weights;
- dimensions and speed of road haulage vehicles in EU member states and non-member countries;
- restrictions imposed on the movement and speeds of road haulage vehicles.

H3.

Be able to draw up drivers' instructions for checking their compliance with the safety requirements concerning the condition of the vehicles, their equipment and cargo, and concerning preventive measures to be taken.

Topics covered:

Write instructions for:
- inspection;
- defect reporting;
- safe use of vehicles and equipment, including cargo.

H4.

Be able to lay down procedures to be followed in the event of an accident and to implement appropriate procedures for preventing the recurrence of accidents or serious traffic offences.

Topics covered:

Accident procedures:
- introduce measures to inform appropriate authorities and personnel of accidents;
- take appropriate action to minimize further dangers and to relieve suffering;
- know the use of European Accident Statements.

Limerick Institute of Technology - LIBRARY
Institiúid Teicneolaíochta Luimnigh - LEABHARLANN
Class No. 629·2844 LOW
ACC.NO. 30335
Date: 4 March 2009

The official examination

Examinations for professional competence in road transport are conducted at approved centres throughout the country on behalf of the official examining body, Oxford Cambridge and RSA Examinations (OCR). Normally, they are held four times a year in March, June, October and December on dates published by OCR, from which a list of the centres and future dates can be obtained.

Examination questions are of two types:

- multiple-choice questions in which a number of alternative answers (usually four) are given, from which the candidate has to choose the correct one; and
- a series of questions or written tasks based on a given case-study scenario, which the candidate needs to read carefully to determine what information the examiner is seeking.

The examinations comprise:

- Module 1 (core), taken by both road haulage and road passenger candidates, which lasts for 30 minutes and comprises 20 multiple-choice questions with a 70 per cent pass mark;
- Module 2 (national road haulage), which lasts for one hour and comprises 40 multiple-choice questions with a pass mark of 70 per cent;
- Module 4 (national road haulage), a case-study examination which lasts 90 minutes, during which the candidate must study a given scenario and answer a variety of questions – these may require a short answer or a longer analytical response, with the need to draw up schedules, and interpret data and numerical calculations;

- Module 6 (international road haulage), which lasts for 60 minutes and comprises two sections:
  - Section A, containing 10–12 questions, each requiring a written direct answer, with a 70 per cent pass mark;
  - Section B, containing usually 3 questions, each requiring a short written response, with a 50 per cent pass mark.

Candidates must pass both of these last sections (A and B) at the same examination sitting to obtain a pass in Module 6. In case readers are wondering, Module 3 is National Road Passenger and Module 5 is International Road Passenger.

AWARD OF CERTIFICATES

Candidates who are successful in achieving Unit One (assessment module 1) and Unit Two (assessment modules 2 and 4) will be awarded a Certificate of Professional Competence in National Road Haulage Operations.

Candidates who are successful in achieving Units One, Two and Three (assessment modules 1, 2, 4 and 6) will be awarded a Certificate of Professional Competence in International Road Haulage Operations.

Certificates meet the requirements of the EU Directive in terms of the wording used and the information presented.

Candidates are not required to pass all of the assessment modules at the same sitting. OCR profile certificates are awarded to candidates who achieve fewer than the total number of assessment modules required for a full certificate. Candidates may resit assessment modules in which they were unsuccessful. When a candidate has achieved all of the required combination of modules, profile certificates may be returned to OCR and replaced by a full certificate of professional competence in national road haulage operations or in international road haulage operations. Both national and international certificates are required to support an international 'O' licence.

Results, reports and certificates will normally be issued to centres within eight weeks of the date of the examination. It is the centre's responsibility to inform individual candidates of their results and to forward certificates where appropriate.

SUGGESTIONS FOR EXAMINEES

Candidates are advised to read the examination questions *very carefully*. While the examinations do not feature 'trick' questions, the examiners do endeavour to set questions with a degree of difficulty to test the candidate's knowledge and intelligence to the full. Thus some questions are not quite as straightforward as they may seem at first glance. The author recommends that candidates should read each question very carefully and then ask themselves 'What am I being asked?' When they are sure they know what the question is really asking, then – and only then – should they look to see what choice of answers they are given.

In the case of multiple-choice questions, where examinees are not sure they know the correct answer to mark, they should consider each given answer in turn and determine whether it could possibly be right. Often two out of the four choices are very wide of the mark and can easily be discounted. This reduces the odds quite considerably for guessing the right answer. Many candidates come out of the examination room kicking themselves because they quickly realize, when it is too late, that they did not read a question carefully enough or properly interpret what they were being asked.

The case-study scenarios and related questions present the candidate with a much more complex form of examination. Here the need is for the scenario to be studied and then careful thought to be given to the implications set by the scenario. For example, where an international operation is described the candidate must think through *all* the implications of such an operation such as the potential CMR liability of the operator and requirements for CMR consignment notes, the value implications for the goods in the event of a claim for loss or damage, customs requirements (eg CT or TIR, 'T' forms, etc), the legal aspects of the driving operation and technical aspects of operating the truck, all the cost implications (including ferries and additional driver costs) and the documentary requirements (eg driving licence/IDP for the driver, registration document for the vehicle, letter of authority, ADR/ATP/ATA requirements, etc), and so on. Missing out basic requirements or key points in any particular scenario will lose vital marks.

Suggestions for the use of this book

Cover up the questions after the one you are currently thinking about, because subsequent questions may give clues to the correct answers to earlier questions.

Do not mark answers in the book: use a separate sheet of paper for this purpose to allow for repeated use of the book.

Finally: *read the questions and scenarios very carefully*. Best of luck!

Typical questions: Civil law

(covering syllabus sections A1 to A4)

INTRODUCTION TO LAW

1. Which of the following is an example of statute law?
   (a) the Road Vehicles (Construction and Use) Regulations 1986
   (b) the Motor Vehicles (Authorization of Special Types) General Order 1979
   (c) the Road Traffic Act 1988
   (d) the Road Vehicles (Registration and Licensing) Regulations 1971

2. Law made by Parliament is called:
   (a) common law
   (b) statute law
   (c) canon law
   (d) case law

3. Which of the following is an example of subordinate legislation?
   (a) a decision made in a court of law
   (b) the Transport Act 1968
   (c) the Goods Vehicles (Plating and Testing) Regulations 1988
   (d) the Health and Safety at Work etc. Act 1974

CONTRACTS

4. To be legally enforceable all contracts must comprise:
   (a) an offer only
   (b) an offer and an acceptance
   (c) an offer, acceptance and consideration
   (d) an offer, acceptance, consideration and confirmation in writing

5. If a court upholds a breach-of-contract action this usually results in:
   (a) the defendant being fined
   (b) the plaintiff receiving an award of damages
   (c) the defendant being given a term of imprisonment
   (d) a ban on both plaintiff and defendant entering into further contracts with each other

6. Which of the following is not necessary for a contract to be legally
   valid?
   (a) the offer
   (b) a consideration
   (c) the acceptance
   (d) confirmation in writing

7. In law a contract legally exists when:
   (a) one party has done all that it contracted to do
   (b) it is confirmed in writing
   (c) both parties have done what they contracted to do
   (d) an offer has been accepted

8. A contract made verbally between parties:
   (a) has no validity in law
   (b) is legally enforceable provided it is confirmed in writing
   (c) would be legally binding in an emergency situation
   (d) is legally binding on the parties concerned

9. In contract terms, an offer is deemed to be accepted when:
   (a) both parties fulfil what they have each contracted to do
   (b) the party accepting an offer has fulfilled what he or she contracted to do
   (c) the person to whom an offer is made accepts the contract terms
   (d) the person to whom an offer is made communicates his or her
   acceptance to the person making the offer

10. Under the law of contract, an offer may be withdrawn at:
    (a) any time
    (b) any time before it is accepted
    (c) any time after it is accepted
    (d) any time providing the withdrawal is made in writing

11. When negotiating contracts, if an offer is made but subject to specified conditions, the offeree must be made aware of those conditions:
    (a) as soon as possible
    (b) at or before the time the contract is made
    (c) no later than 24 hours after the contract is made
    (d) no later than 7 days after the contract is made

12. In contract law, the term 'consideration' is taken to mean that:
    (a) each party must derive a benefit from the contract
    (b) all the parties involved must behave fairly towards each other
    (c) the parties must think carefully before they make the contract
    (d) each party must ensure they interpret the contract terms identically

LEGAL OBLIGATIONS

13. A claim for damages resulting from a haulier's alleged negligence can succeed only if:
    (a) the haulier failed to fulfil a statutory obligation
    (b) the negligence arose from a criminal action
    (c) the haulier had a legally binding contract with the plaintiff
    (d) the plaintiff can show that they have suffered a loss

14. A haulier who accepts haulage work subject to the terms set out in their conditions of carriage restricts their legal liability to that of:
    (a) a common carrier
    (b) a private carrier
    (c) a limited liability carrier
    (d) a public liability carrier

15. Which of the following organizations publishes standard road haulage industry conditions of carriage?
    (a) the Road Haulage Association
    (b) the Freight Transport Association
    (c) the Office of Fair Trading
    (d) the Department of Trade and Industry

16. Road hauliers can legally restrict their liability to their customers by:
    (a) only employing reliable staff under strict conditions of employment
    (b) only accepting haulage work under their published Conditions of Carriage
    (c) making a disclaimer in their company's Articles of Association
    (d) sending to customers a copy of their company's Memorandum of Association

17. A haulage company's conditions of carriage are legally binding provided that:
    (a) copies are sent to the customer after the delivery has been made
    (b) they are printed on the back of collection notes
    (c) the driver carries a copy in their cab
    (d) they are drawn to the attention of customers before contracts for haulage are made

18. Which of the following would not normally be found in standard conditions of carriage?
    (a) specification of the make of vehicles to be used
    (b) specified loading and unloading conditions
    (c) detailed requirements regarding the labelling of goods
    (d) limits on financial liability for loss of or damage to goods

19. Which of the following liability conditions applies to contracts of carriage with both private and common carriers?
    (a) carriers are liable for loss resulting only from their own negligence
    (b) carriers cannot limit their liability except against Acts of God or other 'excepted perils'
    (c) documentary evidence of a contract is not required
    (d) these conditions do not apply to either private or common carriers

20. The rights of carriers to hold goods until they have been paid for their services is legally considered as:
    (a) a bond
    (b) a lien
    (c) a warranty
    (d) a power of detention

21. A private carrier would be held liable for loss of or damage to a customer's goods if it could be proven that it was due to negligence on the part of the:

(a) consignor's staff who inadequately packed the goods
(b) consignor's staff who mis-labelled the goods
(c) consignee
(d) carrier's employees

22. The meaning of the legal term 'particular lien' in relation to road haulage is that:
    (a) the carrier must specify a date when carriage charges are due for payment
    (b) the carrier may detain goods until carriage charges for moving those particular goods are paid
    (c) the carrier may detain the goods carried for a particular period of time until carriage charges are paid
    (d) the carrier may detain any of the owner's goods until all outstanding carriage charges are paid

23. Where a haulier subcontracts work to a third-party haulier and this results in loss of a customer's goods:
    (a) the haulier is liable to the customer for the full amount of the claim
    (b) the haulier would only be liable to meet the customer's claim if the subcontractor failed to do so
    (c) the haulier could not be held liable to the customer in these circumstances
    (d) the haulier cannot be held liable if the customer was informed in advance of the name of the subcontractor who was to transport the goods

24. If a haulier's fleet is fully committed but they still accept additional work
    (a) a contract exists and therefore the work can only be subcontracted at the original price
    (b) a contract exists, so the haulier must still carry out the work
    (c) the haulier may subcontract the work but must inform the subcontracted haulier of the price charged to the customer
    (d) the haulier may subcontract the work without advising the subcontracted haulier of the price charged to the customer

25. A petrol-tanker driver who causes an explosion at a petrol filling station through lighting a cigarette would be considered to be guilty of:
    (a) a breach of their contract of employment
    (b) an act of arson
    (c) criminal negligence
    (d) failing to take due care

26. Vicarious liability means that an employer is responsible for the negligent actions of an employee while the employee is acting within the scope of their authority:
    (a) True
    (b) False

27. A plaintiff's claim for damages as a result of a haulier's negligence could only be successful if:
    (a) the plaintiff has suffered loss or injury
    (b) it could be proved that the haulier had broken the law
    (c) the haulier had entered into a valid legal contract with the plaintiff
    (d) the haulier has committed a criminal offence

28. Where a person suffers injury from the action of an employee in the course of the latter's duties:
    (a) they may sue the employee only
    (b) they may sue the employee's employer only
    (c) they may sue both employee and employer
    (d) as this was an accident that happened at work they cannot sue anyone

29. An occupier of premises owes a common duty of care towards both visitors and employees under the:
    (a) Health and Safety at Work etc. Act 1974
    (b) Landowners' Act 1878
    (c) Employment Protection (Consolidation) Act 1978
    (d) Occupiers Liability Act 1957 (as amended)

30. Occupiers of premises:
    (a) must take reasonable care to safeguard trespassers on their premises
    (b) can set man-traps and use loose guard dogs to deter trespassers
    (c) cannot sue a trespasser even if they cause damage to the premises
    (d) have no legal duty of care towards trespassers

31. A person who is injured when visiting company-owned premises:
    (a) would be able to seek damages if negligence could be proved against the company
    (b) would be able to seek damages only if they were injured as a result of the work activity of an employee at the premises
    (c) would not be able to claim damages if, at the time they sustained injury, they were trespassing on the premises
    (d) would not be able to claim damages against the company under any circumstances

32. A haulier permits a driver to take a vehicle home each night and at weekends, where it remains parked in the street outside the driver's house. Local residents complain that it blocks the street and causes them a private nuisance by depriving them of light. Who in law is liable for the nuisance?
   (a) the driver alone
   (b) the operator alone
   (c) both driver and operator
   (d) there is no liability by either party as the vehicle is parked on a public road

33. Which of the following constitutes a public nuisance?
   (a) causing disturbance to a neighbour with excessive noise late at night
   (b) causing pollution by dumping waste oil on private land
   (c) obstructing the gateway to private land with a vehicle
   (d) blocking a busy street with a lorry which has shed part of its load

34. A haulier who allows smoke from a bonfire on their premises to spoil a neighbour's enjoyment of his or her garden would constitute what form of tort?
   (a) public nuisance
   (b) private nuisance
   (c) trespass
   (d) negligence

35. A haulier whose premises adjoin a row of private houses is sued by one of the householders, who claims that the activities of the firm substantially interfere with his enjoyment of the land which he occupies. If a court upheld the householder's claim, the haulier would be found to have committed the tort of:
   (a) trespass
   (b) public nuisance
   (c) private nuisance
   (d) negligence

36. When goods are sold on a credit–sale arrangement they become the legal property of the purchaser:
   (a) after six months from the date of sale
   (b) when half of the total number of instalments have been paid
   (c) when all instalments have been paid
   (d) when a deposit or the first instalment has been paid

37. Road hauliers can restrict their legal liability by defining the limits of their liability in their:
    (a) Articles of Association
    (b) Memorandum of Association
    (c) contracts of employment
    (d) conditions of carriage

38. By accepting haulage contracts subject to the terms laid down in their conditions of carriage, operators restricts their legal liability to that of:
    (a) a public carrier
    (b) a common carrier
    (c) a corporate carrier
    (d) a private carrier

PRINCIPALS AND SUBCONTRACTORS

39. In business relationships, which of the following is not legally considered to be an agent?
    (a) a factor
    (b) a broker
    (c) a principal
    (d) an auctioneer

40. An authorized agent acting on commission for a haulier arranged for collection and delivery of a customer's goods, but – due to over-booking by the haulier – the customer's schedules could not be met and the customer claims substantial losses as a result of this. How do the parties legally stand?
    (a) the customer can sue the agent for their own losses
    (b) the customer can sue the haulier alone for their own losses in full
    (c) the customer can sue both the haulier and the agent jointly for any loss
    (d) there can be no claim as this is one of the hazards of using hauliers

41. When a contract is made by an agent on behalf of their principal, this contract is binding on:
    (a) both the agent and the third party
    (b) both the principal and their agent
    (c) both the principal and the third party
    (d) the principal, the agent and the third party

42. If an authorized agent makes secret profits from business dealings with customers on behalf of the agent's principal:
    (a) the principal can sue the agent for an amount equal to those profits
    (b) the agent can keep the profits whether or not the principal suffered any loss
    (c) the profits must be returned to the customers from whom they were obtained
    (d) the agent may keep the profits so long as the principal suffered no loss

CMR LIABILITY

43. An international road haulier should take out insurance cover against:
    (a) consequential loss of goods en route
    (b) CMR liabilities
    (c) goods-in-transit risks
    (d) Customs claims for unpaid duty

44. A UK haulier transporting a hire-or-reward load from Leeds to Bordeaux via the cross-channel ferries would be subject to CMR Convention conditions:
    (a) only if they voluntarily agree to accept the conditions
    (b) only for that part of the journey on mainland Europe
    (c) for the whole of the journey
    (d) only if they have taken out CMR liability insurance cover

45. When transporting goods by road for hire or reward on an international journey, goods-in-transit insurance should be obtained to:
    (a) cover maximum liabilities of £800 per tonne
    (b) cover maximum liabilities of £1,200 per tonne
    (c) cover the current level of CMR liability
    (d) cover liabilities in the currency of the country of destination

CHAPTER 5

Typical questions: Commercial law

(covering syllabus sections B1 and B2)

TRADING LAW

46. A partnership would automatically be dissolved if:
    (a) any one of the partners died or became bankrupt
    (b) any one of the partners said they were resigning
    (c) any one of the partners was unable or unwilling to continue working
    (d) one partner sacked the other partners

47. If a person intends trading as a road haulier under a name other than their own they must:
    (a) notify the Department of the Environment, Transport and the Regions
    (b) register the name with the Department of Trade and Industry
    (c) display their own name and the trading name at their place of business
    (d) register the trading name with the Registrar of Business Names

48. Where two or more persons enter into a partnership arrangement:
    (a) individual partners are responsible only for their own personal actions

(b) partners may legally negotiate individual business contracts with the partnership

(c) the action of each individual partner is legally binding on the other partners

(d) individual partners are not legally empowered to act for the partnership without the specific authority of the other partners

49. A partner in a haulage firm is:
   (a) personally liable for all debts incurred by the partnership
   (b) not personally liable for any business debt incurred by the partnership
   (c) liable only for a proportion of the debts in accordance with their own partnership share
   (d) not liable for business debts incurred by their partners without their knowledge

50. Any business, apart from a public limited company, which trades as a registered company must, under the provisions of the Companies Act, have a name ending with:
   (a) incorporated
   (b) company
   (c) limited
   (d) plc

51. When a private limited company wishes to increase its share capital under the provisions of the Companies Act, it may:
   (a) not advertise for the public to subscribe for shares
   (b) advertise the availability of shares to the public
   (c) publicly offer to exchange new shares for capital investment
   (d) not offer any share holding beyond the existing shareholders

COMPANY LAW

52. A private limited company must have at least:
   (a) one shareholder
   (b) two shareholders
   (c) four shareholders
   (d) seven shareholders

53. The term 'share capital' is used in company law to mean:
   (a) the share of business profits paid to shareholders in dividends
   (b) the capital invested in a company by its shareholders
   (c) the method for allocating dividends among shareholders
   (d) the total capital employed as shown in the balance sheet

54. To enable a newly registered limited liability company to operate legally, it must have the minimum number of shareholders and they must sign:
    (a) the Declaration of Incorporation
    (b) the Articles of Association
    (c) the Memorandum of Association
    (d) a Certificate of Incorporation

55. When a limited liability company is to be prosecuted for an offence, this is addressed to and answerable by:
    (a) the company secretary
    (b) the chairman
    (c) the managing director
    (d) the board of directors collectively

56. The objects of a company are set out in its:
    (a) Certificate of Incorporation
    (b) Annual Report
    (c) Articles of Association
    (d) Memorandum of Association

57. A recently formed limited liability company is required to hold its first Annual General Meeting (AGM) of members within:
    (a) 6 months
    (b) 12 months
    (c) 18 months
    (d) 24 months

58. A written notice of the annual general meeting for a company must be sent to all members at least:
    (a) 7 days in advance
    (b) 14 days in advance
    (c) 21 days in advance
    (d) 28 days in advance

59. Which type of general meeting could be called by a quorum of shareholders in a limited liability company to discuss an important business matter?
    (a) a board meeting
    (b) an Annual General Meeting
    (c) a directors' meeting
    (d) an extraordinary general meeting

60. What minimum number of shareholder members of a public limited company must sign the company's Memorandum of Association?
    (a) 2
    (b) 3
    (c) 7
    (d) 12

61. The legal statement of the purposes for which a private limited liability company is established and of the liability of its members is called:
    (a) the Register
    (b) a Certificate of Incorporation
    (c) the Memorandum of Association
    (d) the Articles of Association

62. The Articles of Association of a limited liability company is a document:
    (a) containing a list of all shareholders' names
    (b) sent by way of a prospectus to potential shareholders in the company
    (c) setting out the objects for which the company was established
    (d) setting out the rules governing the internal working of the company

63. A public limited company must have a name ending with the letters or words:
    (a) company limited
    (b) limited
    (c) plc
    (d) incorporated

64. A public limited company is required to have at least:
    (a) 2 members
    (b) 7 members
    (c) 10 members
    (d) 100 members

65. A public limited company must have a minimum authorized share capital of at least:
    (a) £1,000
    (b) £50,000
    (c) £500,000
    (d) £1,000,000

66. Under the provisions of the Companies Act, company directors are required to have specific regard to the interests of:
    (a) the shareholders only
    (b) both employees and shareholders
    (c) employees only
    (d) employees, shareholders and suppliers

67. The legal requirement for companies to produce detailed audited accounts does not apply in firms that have an annual turnover:
    (a) not exceeding £100,000
    (b) not exceeding £350,000
    (c) not exceeding £250,000
    (d) exceeding £350,000

68. Which of the following classes of shareholder always has voting rights in a company?
    (a) ordinary shareholders
    (b) preference shareholders
    (c) debenture holders
    (d) shareholder directors

69. The statutory rights of shareholders in a limited liability company are to be found in the:
    (a) Annual Report
    (b) Certificate of Incorporation
    (c) Memorandum of Association
    (d) Articles of Association

70. If a creditor obtains a company winding-up order from a court the resulting action on the part of the company would be called:
    (a) a statutory meeting of creditors
    (b) voluntary liquidation
    (c) compulsory liquidation
    (d) declaration of bankruptcy

CHAPTER 6

Typical questions: Social law

(covering syllabus sections C1 to C4)

TRIBUNALS AND TRADE UNIONS

71. The Advisory, Conciliation and Arbitration Service (ACAS) is:
    (a) an agency of the TUC
    (b) a department within the Department of Education and Employment
    (c) a statutory body
    (d) a department of the CBI

72. The role of the Advisory, Conciliation and Arbitration Service is to:
    (a) represent trade unions in dispute with company management
    (b) represent employees in dispute with employers
    (c) resolve issues between employers and employees in dispute
    (d) offer advice to employees, employers, trade associations and trade unions

73. If ACAS cannot settle a dispute, the next legal step that can be taken is:
    (a) to refer the matter to the CAC
    (b) to refer the matter to the Traffic Commissioner
    (c) to refer the matter to the Department of Trade and Industry
    (d) no further action

74. The Trade Union and Labour Relations (Consolidation) Act 1992 gives employees which of the following rights regarding union membership?
    (a) no right to belong to a trade union
    (b) no rights either to belong or not to belong to a trade union
    (c) a right to belong or not to belong to a trade union
    (d) a right to belong but no right not to belong to a trade union

75. Under the Trade Union and Labour Relations (Consolidation) Act 1992 it is illegal for employers to discriminate against employees on the grounds of trade union membership.
    (a) True
    (b) False

76. The Central Arbitration Committee was set up to deal with complaints about:
    (a) appeals against unfair dismissal
    (b) failure by an employer to recognize an independent trade union
    (c) failure by an employer to disclose information
    (d) unfair contract of employment terms

EMPLOYMENT LAW

77. Industrial action ballots must be fully postal under which of the following Acts?
    (a) Trade Union Reform and Employment Rights Act 1993
    (b) Employment Protection Act 1975
    (c) Trade Union and Labour Relations Act 1974
    (d) Contracts of Employment Act 1972

78. Under employment law a full-time worker is one who works more than:
    (a) 10 hours per week
    (b) 12 hours per week
    (c) 16 hours per week
    (d) 24 hours per week

79. Picketing in furtherance of a trade dispute is legally permitted so long as:
    (a) it peacefully attempts to persuade employees to work or not work
    (b) it prevents employees only from entering the work premises
    (c) it takes place only on the employer's premises
    (d) the police have given specific permission for it to take place

80. Secondary action in furtherance of a trade dispute is action taken:
    (a) in sympathy with a strike
    (b) to induce a person to break a contract of employment
    (c) against customers of the employer with whom the dispute exists
    (d) against employees who are not involved in the dispute

81. An employee is entitled to at least one week's notice of dismissal after completing:
    (a) 4 weeks' service
    (b) 12 weeks' service
    (c) 13 weeks' service
    (d) 26 weeks' service

82. An employee wishing to end their employment must give at least one week's notice:
    (a) after being employed for one week
    (b) after being employed for two weeks or more
    (c) after being employed for one month or more
    (d) irrespective of how long they have been employed

83. How much notice of termination of employment is an employee with 5 years and 11 months' continuous service entitled to receive from their employer? Is it:
    (a) 3 weeks
    (b) 4 weeks
    (c) 5 weeks
    (d) 6 weeks

84. Employers must show that dismissal of an employee was reasonable in all the circumstances. Is this:
    (a) True
    (b) False

85. Firms established for less than 2 years and employing fewer than a certain number of people are exempted from the unfair dismissal provisions. The relevant number of employees is:
    (a) 5
    (b) 12
    (c) 18
    (d) 20

86. The statutory time limit within which a dismissed employee can make an unfair dismissal claim to an employment tribunal is:
    (a) 6 months
    (b) 3 months
    (c) 2 months
    (d) 1 month

87. A claim to an employment tribunal for unfair dismissal cannot be made unless the employee has completed a minimum of:
    (a) 13 weeks' service
    (b) 26 weeks' service
    (c) 52 weeks' service
    (d) 104 weeks' service

88. An employee who is dismissed after completing at least 4 weeks continuous service with an employer:
    (a) is not entitled to a written statement of the reasons for dismissal
    (b) is not entitled to a written statement if dismissed for misconduct
    (c) must be given a written statement of the reasons on request
    (d) must always be given a written statement of the reasons for dismissal

89. In a claim before an employment tribunal for unfair dismissal, the burden of proof as to whether the dismissal was fair or unfair rests with:
    (a) ACAS
    (b) the employer only
    (c) both the employer and the employee
    (d) the dismissed person

90. An employee who has been dismissed is entitled to a written reason for dismissal:
    (a) irrespective of the reasons for dismissal
    (b) under no circumstances
    (c) only if the employee specifically requests it
    (d) only if the employee has at least 2 years' service with the employer

91. Where a person claims that dismissal was due to trade union membership and activities, the industrial tribunal accepting the complaint would:
    (a) order reinstatement or re-engagement only
    (b) order reinstatement or re-engagement and make a 'special' award
    (c) make a basic award only
    (d) make a compensatory award only

92. Which of the following employees may claim unfair dismissal?
    (a) a man aged 25 years with 3 years' continuous employment
    (b) a woman aged 62 with 11 years' continuous employment
    (c) a part-time employee
    (d) an employee who normally works overseas

93. Which of the following is an unfair reason for dismissal?
    (a) the employee's conduct
    (b) being a member of a trade union
    (c) the lack of suitable qualifications
    (d) where a particular job becomes redundant

94. When an employer plans to make between 10 and 99 employees redundant over a period of 30 days, the Secretary of State for Employment must be notified at least:
    (a) 10 days in advance
    (b) 30 days in advance
    (c) 60 days in advance
    (d) 90 days in advance

95. Which of the following persons made redundant would be eligible to claim statutory redundancy payment?
    (a) an employee aged 20 and employed continuously for 3 years
    (b) an employee aged 32 and employed continuously for 18 months
    (c) a man aged 64 and employed continuously for 5 years
    (d) a woman aged 60 and employed continuously for 25 years

96. Which of the following persons would not be entitled to a statutory redundancy payment?
    (a) a man aged 28 with 18 months' service with his employer
    (b) a woman aged 20 with 2 years' service with her employer
    (c) a man aged 64 with 3 years' service with his employer
    (d) a woman aged 59 with 10 years' service with her employer

97. Which of the following employees is entitled to a redundancy payment?
    (a) a part-timer with 2 years' service working 12 hours weekly
    (b) a female senior executive aged 61 years
    (c) a full-timer with 3 years' continuous service
    (d) a person who is self-employed

98. A redundant employee who refuses a reasonable offer of suitable alternative employment with a subsidiary of their present employer would not be entitled to a redundancy payment:
    (a) True
    (b) False

99. Redundancy payments are calculated on the basis of:
    (a) length of service, and sex
    (b) age, length of service and weekly earnings
    (c) weekly earnings only
    (d) sex, age and length of service

100. In calculating a statutory redundancy payment, qualifying service over the age of 22 years and under 41 years counts for payment at a rate of:
    (a) half of one week's pay for each complete year of service
    (b) one week's pay for each complete year of service
    (c) 1.5 weeks' pay for each complete year of service
    (d) two weeks' pay for each complete year of service

101. A person employed by a firm for 1 year and 11 months who is made redundant would be entitled to a statutory minimum period of notice of:
    (a) 1 week
    (b) 2 weeks
    (c) 3 weeks
    (d) 4 weeks

102. When calculating an employee's continuous service for the purposes of determining a redundancy payment, any time they were on strike is:
    (a) included only if the total service exceeds 2 years
    (b) included in the total period of continuous service
    (c) included providing the strike was recognized by a trade union
    (d) not included in the total period of continuous service

103. The maximum period of continuous service with an employer that can be taken into account when calculating redundancy pay is:
    (a) 5 years
    (b) 10 years
    (c) 15 years
    (d) 20 years

104. An employer intending to create 10 or more redundancies within a 30-day period must notify the Employment Secretary and a recognized trade union in advance within a period of:
    (a) 30 days
    (b) 60 days
    (c) 90 days
    (d) 100 days

105. Unlawful industrial action taken by a trade union may result in damages having to be paid by the union. In the case of a union with between 25,000 and 99,999 members these damages are subject to a maximum amount of:
    (a) £10,000
    (b) £50,000
    (c) £125,000
    (d) £250,000

106. If an employer refuses to disclose information to a union under the terms of employment legislation when requested to do so, the union can make a complaint to:
    (a) the RHA
    (b) ACAS
    (c) the CAC
    (d) the TUC

107. What information must legally be disclosed to a recognized trade union within a firm under current employment legislation?
    (a) all information requested
    (b) details of the firm's future investment plans
    (c) personal details of employees' ages and rates of pay
    (d) information necessary for use in collective pay bargaining

108. What information need an employer not disclose to a trade union under consultative procedures for dealing with redundancies?
    (a) the method used for selecting employees for redundancy
    (b) the reasons for creating the redundancies
    (c) the total number of persons employed at the establishment
    (d) amounts to be paid in redundancy payments

109. Which of the following persons would be entitled under employment legislation to time off work with pay to carry out particular duties?
    (a) a shop steward engaging in union business
    (b) a union member wishing to attend a union meeting
    (c) a person called up for jury service
    (d) a Justice of the Peace to carry out their public duties

110. An employee who is an official of his local trade union branch can claim time off work for training in connection with those duties amounting to:
    (a) up to 1 hour each day
    (b) up to 3 days per week
    (c) 4 days per week
    (d) any amount of time that is reasonably necessary

111. Under employment legislation an official of an independent trade union is entitled to time off work with pay for the purposes of:
    (a) attending local council meetings in their role as a local councillor
    (b) attending official trade union duties and training
    (c) undertaking their duties as a Justice of the Peace
    (d) attending to official trade union duties only

112. An employee who is on the committee of a local educational establishment and has to attend occasional meetings during normal working hours:
    (a) may have a reasonable amount of unpaid time off to attend meetings
    (b) may have a reasonable amount of time off with pay to attend such meetings
    (c) need not be given any time off to attend the meetings
    (d) is only entitled to time off to attend meetings if they work extra time to compensate the employer for their absence

113. Which of the following benefits is not within the scope of Wages Council orders?
    (a) employees' remuneration
    (b) workers' holiday entitlements
    (c) company manning levels
    (d) conditions of employment

114. A contract of employment between an employer and employee exists:
    (a) only if the offer of employment and acceptance are in writing
    (b) when the employee receives a written statement of the terms and conditions of employment
    (c) when the employer offers employment which is accepted by the employee
    (d) once the employee has worked continuously for a period of 4 weeks

115. Which of the following terms should be included in a contract of employment?
(a) the employee's national insurance number
(b) the periods of notice required on termination of the employment
(c) the employee's educational and job qualifications
(d) details of the employee's interests and hobbies

116. An employer has a statutory duty to give a new employee a written statement of the main terms and conditions of their employment:
(a) prior to commencing the employment
(b) immediately on commencing the employment
(c) within 4 weeks of commencing the employment
(d) within 2 months of commencing the employment

117. If an employee's terms of employment are changed, they must be notified within what statutory period of time?
(a) 3 weeks
(b) 1 month
(c) 13 weeks
(d) 3 months

118. An employee suspended from work for medical reasons may be entitled to full pay for:
(a) at least 4 weeks
(b) 13 weeks
(c) 26 weeks
(d) 1 year

119. Female employees wishing to return to work early after confinement must advise their employers of this fact in writing and give:
(a) 7 days' notice
(b) 14 days' notice
(c) 21 days' notice
(d) 28 days' notice

120. A female employee who is pregnant is:
(a) entitled to receive time off without pay for antenatal examinations
(b) entitled to receive time off with pay for antenatal examinations
(c) entitled to receive a reasonable amount of time off to receive antenatal care but must make up this time later
(d) not entitled to any time off for antenatal care

121. A woman who is claiming maternity leave normally has a right to return to work up to:
    (a) 29 weeks after her confinement
    (b) 49 weeks after her confinement
    (c) 52 weeks after her confinement
    (d) 58 weeks after her confinement

122. The Industrial Training Act 1982 deals with:
    (a) building industrial estates to provide employment
    (b) training employees engaged in industry
    (c) the winding-up of most of the industrial training boards
    (d) formulating industrial relations policies

123. What official body is responsible for providing the policy framework within which the TECs operate
    (a) the Department for Education and Employment
    (b) the Advisory, Conciliation and Arbitration Service
    (c) the Training, Enterprise and Education Directorate
    (d) the Manpower Services Commission

124. What National Insurance contributions are payable by a self-employed person?
    (a) Class 1 contributions
    (b) Class 3 contributions
    (c) Classes 2 and 4 contributions
    (d) no contributions

125. Which of the following benefits is dependent upon an employee having paid a certain number of National Insurance contributions?
    (a) unemployment benefit
    (b) statutory sick pay (SSP)
    (c) supplementary benefit
    (d) family income support

126. Which of the following benefits is not available to a self-employed person?
    (a) maternity allowance
    (b) widow's pension
    (c) unemployment benefit
    (d) sickness benefit

127. A person who loses their job as a result of alleged misconduct could be disqualified from claiming unemployment benefit for a period:
    (a) True
    (b) False

128. To qualify for SSP an employee must be absent from work for at least:
    (a) 1 complete qualifying day
    (b) 2 complete qualifying days
    (c) 3 complete qualifying days
    (d) 4 complete qualifying days

129. The maximum entitlement for SSP in any period of incapacity for work is:
    (a) 1 week
    (b) 4 weeks
    (c) 28 weeks
    (d) 52 weeks

130. An employee who is absent from work through illness for ten days continuously, under the Statutory Sick Pay scheme must be paid sickness benefit for:
    (a) 2 days
    (b) 3 days
    (c) 7 days
    (d) 10 days

131. Under the SSP scheme a 'small' employer may claim back sickness payments:
    (a) by deduction from the employer's payments to the VAT office
    (b) from the Department of Social Security
    (c) by deduction from the National Insurance contributions
    (d) from the Secretary of State for Health

132. Under the two-tier state pension scheme an additional pension is paid according to:
    (a) the number of years' contributions paid into the scheme
    (b) the length of service with the final employer
    (c) the total number of years in paid employment
    (d) the type of private pension scheme operated by the employer

133. Racial discrimination is not prohibited by the Race Relations Act 1976:
    (a) in the training of employees
    (b) in the recruitment of company management
    (c) where employees work in private households
    (d) in meeting the special educational needs of particular racial groups

134. A person subjected to racial discrimination by being refused credit sale facilities would need to complain to:
    (a) the county or sheriff's court
    (b) an industrial tribunal
    (c) the Office of Fair Trading
    (d) the Commission on Racial Equality

135. It would be lawful for an employer to pay a male employee at a higher rate than a female employee for doing the same or similar work where:
    (a) the man had been employed for a longer period than the woman
    (b) the man is older than the woman
    (c) the man is married and the woman is single
    (d) they are of different ethnic origins

136. A female employee claiming equal pay for a particular job must be able to establish that:
    (a) she is a full-time employee
    (b) she has been doing the particular job for at least 12 months
    (c) the job she does is the same as or broadly similar to those done by the male employees
    (d) her educational qualifications are equal to those of the male employees

137. An employee who feels discriminated against on the grounds of his or her sex can make a complaint to:
    (a) the police
    (b) the Equal Opportunities Commission
    (c) an employment tribunal
    (d) the Employment Appeals Tribunal

138. Sex discrimination between the sexes is prohibited in the case of:
    (a) recruitment of a matron for a girls' school
    (b) recruitment of a cook to work in a private household
    (c) recruitment of a telephonist/receptionist for a firm
    (d) when seeking fashion models

139. A haulier could advertise under the Sex Discrimination Act for:
     (a) a mature female word-processor operator
     (b) a strong lad for warehouse duties
     (c) an attractive young lady receptionist
     (d) an LGV driver (male or female applicants considered)

140. Which of the following advertisements would be lawful under Sex Discrimination legislation?
     (a) male washroom attendant wanted
     (b) young lady wanted for typing pool
     (c) warehousemen required
     (d) tea lady required

141. The register of disabled persons is maintained by the:
     (a) local office of the Department of Social Security
     (b) Area Health Authority
     (c) Department for Education and Employment
     (d) Manpower Services Commission

142. The Disability Discrimination Act 1995 applies to employers who:
     (a) have 15 or more employees
     (b) have 25 or more employees
     (c) are a public limited company
     (d) are registered with the Manpower Services Commission

143. Employers who provide goods or services must make allowance for disabled persons by:
     (a) employing a minimum number of such persons
     (b) providing a specified number of disabled toilets
     (c) making reasonable adjustments to premises to ensure access for such persons
     (d) rebuild their premises to facilitate wheelchair access

144. An employee may take an equal-pay complaint to an employment tribunal while still employed or within:
     (a) 6 months of termination of employment
     (b) 9 months of termination of employment
     (c) 12 months of termination of employment
     (d) an unlimited period of time

145. An employee can make a complaint to an employment tribunal on grounds of unfair dismissal within:
     (a) 1 month from the date of dismissal
     (b) 2 months from the date of dismissal

(c) 3 months from the date the dismissal took effect

(d) not until 6 months have elapsed since the date of dismissal

146. An employee of a firm employing not more than 20 employees claiming for unfair dismissal to an employment tribunal must have been employed continuously for at least:
(a) 13 weeks
(b) 26 weeks
(c) 52 weeks
(d) 104 weeks

147. Which of the following types of employment complaint would not be dealt with by an employment tribunal?
(a) unfair dismissal
(b) redundancy disputes
(c) complaints regarding sex discrimination
(d) claims for industrial injury benefit

HEALTH AND SAFETY

148. The principal object of the Factories Act is to:
(a) control the hours during which factories may operate
(b) regulate the way in which factories are built
(c) ensure the health, safety and welfare of those who work in factories
(d) lay down statutory minimum rates of pay for factory workers

149. Health and Safety at Work inspectors may enter premises as necessary to enforce the law:
(a) only if accompanied by a police officer
(b) at any time
(c) at any reasonable time
(d) only after serving a notice on the occupier 24 hours in advance

150. If a Health and Safety inspector considers that the work activities being carried out by an employer involve the immediate risk of serious personal injury to employees, the inspector may issue:
(a) a notice of intended prosecution
(b) a health and safety contravention notice
(c) an improvement notice
(d) a prohibition notice

151. When a Health and Safety inspector issues an improvement notice the working practice to which it refers:
    (a) must stop immediately until an improvement is made
    (b) may continue provided the improvement is made within the specified time limit
    (c) must not continue, and failure to carry out the improvement will result in prosecution
    (d) may continue provided that a safety representative supervises the work

152. A fire certificate is legally required:
    (a) in all works premises and offices
    (b) for premises where petroleum products are used or stored
    (c) if more than 20 people are employed in total or more than 10 are employed above ground floor
    (d) to confirm that firms have adequate fire insurance cover

153. Safety representatives at a place of work are appointed by:
    (a) the firm's managing director
    (b) the company secretary
    (c) the shop stewards
    (d) trade union members employed in the firm

154. A person appointed as a safety representative should have been employed in that firm or in similar employment elsewhere for a minimum of:
    (a) 1 year
    (b) 2 years
    (c) 3 years
    (d) 4 years

155. Apart from domestic employees, the maximum number of persons who may be employed before a written safety policy must be produced is:
    (a) 2
    (b) 3
    (c) 5
    (d) 10

156. A qualified first-aider must be appointed when a firm employs more than:
    (a) 10 people
    (b) 50 people
    (c) 100 people
    (d) 150 people

157. In high-hazard industrial establishments, a first-aid room should be provided, and in premises where:
   (a) more than 50 people are employed
   (b) more than 100 people are employed
   (c) more than 250 people are employed
   (d) more than 400 people are employed

158. Where the walls of a factory or workshop have 'smooth impervious surfaces' they must be washed with hot water and soap or cleaned by some other approved method once every:
   (a) 12 months
   (b) 14 months
   (c) 24 months
   (d) 7 years

159. Under the provisions of the Factories Act, factory walls which are painted or varnished must be repainted every:
   (a) 14 months
   (b) 5 years
   (c) 7 years
   (d) 10 years

160. Where a substantial amount of work in a work room involves sitting down and requires little physical effort, the temperature after the first hour must be not less than:
   (a) 15 degrees Centigrade
   (b) 16 degrees Centigrade
   (c) 18 degrees Centigrade
   (d) 66 degrees Fahrenheit

161. The Factories Act requires air receivers to be examined by a competent person every:
   (a) 6 months
   (b) 12 months
   (c) 24 months
   (d) 26 months

162. The Factories Act requires cranes used in industrial premises to be examined by a competent person once every:
   (a) 6 months
   (b) 12 months
   (c) 14 months
   (d) 18 months

163. The Factories Act specifies minimum numbers of separate toilet facilities for male and female employees. How many toilets would need to be provided where there are 75 male employees and two female employees?
    (a) 3 male plus 1 female
    (b) 4 male plus 2 female
    (c) 2 male plus 2 female
    (d) 4 male plus 2 female and 1 for visitors

164. Where a serious work accident falls within the scope of the RID-DOR regulations this has to be reported:
    (a) immediately by telephone
    (b) immediately by telephone followed in writing within 7 days
    (c) in writing within 7 days
    (d) only if the injured person subsequently dies

165. Reports on accidents involving death or injury during loading, unloading or the conveyance of dangerous chemicals must be made to:
    (a) the police
    (b) the Goods Vehicle Traffic Commissioner
    (c) the Health and Safety Executive
    (d) the Department of Health

DRIVERS' HOURS AND RECORDS

166. The maximum time that a driver engaged on UK domestic work can be on duty in one week is:
    (a) 48 hours
    (b) 55 hours
    (c) 60 hours
    (d) 77 hours

167. Under EU Regulations the maximum aggregated driving permitted before a statutory break must be taken is:
    (a) 4 hours
    (b) 4.5 hours
    (c) 5 hours
    (d) 8 hours

168. Regulation 3820/85/EEC, which limits driving to a normal maximum of 9 hours daily, permits an extension to:
    (a) 10 hours on 2 days in any 7-day period
    (b) 10 hours on any 2 days in a week
    (c) 11 hours on 2 days in a week if the extra time is compensated
    (d) 13 hours on 2 days so long as 11-hours' daily rest is taken

169. The maximum that a driver can spend behind the wheel in any one week under EU rules is:
    (a) 36 hours
    (b) 54 hours
    (c) 60 hours
    (d) 6 daily driving shifts

170. If a driver spends 45 hours behind the wheel in one week under EU rules, how many hours can they spend driving during the next following fixed week?
    (a) 34 hours
    (b) 45 hours
    (c) 54 hours
    (d) 56 hours

171. Under Regulation 3820/85 EEC a driver is restricted to a 2-weekly driving limit of:
    (a) 90 hours
    (b) 92 hours
    (c) 102 hours
    (d) 104 hours

172. Current EU rules restrict the maximum working time for a 2-man vehicle crew by setting a minimum rest period requirement of:
    (a) 10 hours each in 27 hours
    (b) 8 hours each in 30 hours
    (c) 11 hours each in 24 hours
    (d) 22 hours between them

173. Under Regulation 3820/85 EEC the driver's statutory minimum break period may be spread throughout the driving period and taken as other breaks of:
    (a) at least 20 minutes each
    (b) at least 30 minutes each
    (c) at least 45 minutes each
    (d) at least 15 minutes each

174. If a driver of a vehicle within the scope of the EU rules starts work at 8.00 am and drives continuously until 12.30 pm, they must then:
    (a) take a break of 20 minutes
    (b) take a single break of half an hour and another break later that day
    (c) take a single break of three-quarters of an hour
    (d) take a break of 20 minutes with two further breaks of 20 minutes each

175. A driver starting a journey at 6.00 am takes a 15-minute break at 8.00 am, then continues driving. To comply with EU rules they must take a further 30-minute break at:
    (a) 10.30 am
    (b) 10.45 am
    (c) 11.00 am
    (d) 11.45 am

176. A driver came on duty at 07.00 hours, loaded their vehicle, and at 08.30 commenced their journey. Under current EU Regulations, if they drove continuously they would have to take a 45-minute break starting not later than:
    (a) 11.30 hours
    (b) 12.30 hours
    (c) 13.00 hours
    (d) 14.00 hours

177. EU Regulations permit a driver to replace the 45-minute mandatory break with:
    (a) 2 breaks of at least 15 minutes each during the driving period
    (b) 3 breaks of at least 15 minutes each taken during the day
    (c) 3 breaks of at least 20 minutes each
    (d) other breaks of at least 15 minutes each, totalling 45 minutes

178. Provisions in the EU drivers' hours rules allow national exemption for vehicles operating exclusively on islands having an area not exceeding:
    (a) 1,000 square miles
    (b) 2,000 square kilometres
    (c) 2,300 square kilometres
    (d) 2,300 square miles

179. Emergency provisions in the EU rules permit a driver to depart from:
   (a) the daily and weekly driving limits only
   (b) both daily and weekly rest period requirements
   (c) both driving limits and rest period requirements
   (d) none of the statutory driving or rest period requirements

180. Which of the following goods vehicles is subject to drivers' hours rules under Regulation 3820/85/EEC?
   (a) a vehicle with a maximum permissible weight of 3.5 tonnes
   (b) a vehicle with a maximum permissible weight exceeding 3.5 tonnes
   (c) a gas board vehicle with a maximum permissible weight of 7.5 tonnes
   (d) a vehicle used for milk collection from farms

181. A driver of a goods vehicle with a permissible maximum weight of 7.5 tonnes, when driving within the UK is subject to:
   (a) the national drivers' hours rules
   (b) the British domestic drivers' hours rules
   (c) the EU drivers' hours rules
   (d) no limit on their driving times

182. A 'day' for the purposes of the EU drivers' hours rules is defined as:
   (a) the period from midnight to midnight
   (b) a period of 24 hours counted from the time of clocking on
   (c) a period of 24 hours preceding any time spent driving
   (d) any period of 24 hours following a daily/weekly rest period

183. A 'week' for the purposes of the EU drivers' hours rules is defined as:
   (a) any period of seven consecutive working days
   (b) the period from 00.00 on Monday to 24.00 on the following Sunday
   (c) from midnight Sunday until midnight on the following Sunday
   (d) any consecutive 6-day period during which a driver works

184. The normal minimum daily rest requirement under EU rules is:
   (a) 10 hours
   (b) 11 hours
   (c) 12 hours
   (d) 13 hours

185. The minimum uninterrupted period that may be counted as daily rest under EU rules is:
(a) 15 minutes
(b) 30 minutes
(c) 1 hour
(d) 2 hours

186. For the past week a driver has taken the full 11-hour daily rest period. On a 2-day journey away from base they may take a daily rest period of not less than:
(a) 8 hours
(b) 9 hours
(c) 10 hours
(d) 11 hours

187. Regulation 3820/85/EEC requires the driver of a double-manned vehicle to have a minimum daily rest period of at least:
(a) 27 hours
(b) 8 hours in the past 30 hours
(c) 9 hours in the past 30 hours
(d) 8 hours in the past 27 hours

188. When a daily rest period under EU rules is not reduced it may be split into two or three periods, one of which must be at least:
(a) 6 hours
(b) 7 hours
(c) 8 hours
(d) 9 hours

189. Under EU rules daily rest periods may be reduced to:
(a) 9 hours on 3 occasions in a week
(b) 9 hours on 2 occasions in 7 days
(c) 8 hours on 3 occasions in a week
(d) 8 hours on 2 occasions in 7 days

190. When reduced daily rest periods have been taken on two occasions in the current week these reductions must be compensated:
(a) in the same week
(b) by the end of the next following week
(c) before the end of the third following week
(d) before the end of the fourth following week

191. Compensated daily and weekly rest must be attached to other rest periods of at least:
(a) 11 hours
(b) 10 hours
(c) 9 hours
(d) 8 hours

192. Which of the following vehicles would be exempt from EU rules and subject to British domestic rules?
(a) a vehicle having a permissible maximum weight of 3.5 tonnes
(b) a vehicle having a permissible maximum weight of 7.5 tonnes
(c) a vehicle having a permissible maximum weight of 2.5 tonnes towing a trailer with a permissible maximum weight of 1,500 kg
(d) a vehicle having a permissible maximum weight of 3 tonnes towing a trailer with a permissible maximum weight of 600 kg

193. Under British domestic rules a driver is allowed to drive for a maximum daily period of:
(a) 10 hours
(b) 11 hours
(c) 12 hours
(d) 12.5 hours

194. If a driver operating under British domestic rules finishes an 11-hour duty shift at 6.00 pm, what is the earliest time they can start work the next day?
(a) 4.00 am
(b) 5.00 am
(c) 6.00 am
(d) 7.00 am

195. A driver employed solely on British domestic work is restricted to a maximum time on duty in any working week of:
(a) 54 hours
(b) 60 hours
(c) 77 hours
(d) 92 hours

196. Under the British domestic drivers' hours regulations, 'driving' means:
(a) time spent with the engine running and the vehicle in motion
(b) time spent with the vehicle in motion and carrying a load
(c) time spent at the wheel with the engine running whether the vehicle is moving or not
(d) time spent between starting and finishing work for the day

197. A medical practitioner using a van for professional purposes under the British domestic drivers' hours regulations is subject to:
(a) daily duty limits only
(b) daily driving limits only
(c) both daily duty and daily driving limits
(d) no limits on their daily driving and duty times

198. If a delivery vehicle under 3.5 tonnes permissible maximum weight does not need an 'O' licence, what record-keeping requirements apply to the driver?
(a) they must use a tachograph to produce records
(b) they must use a domestic driver's record book
(c) they must keep a note of their driving on a time sheet
(d) they are not legally required to keep records

199. A driver of a vehicle exempt from the EU rules must complete a record sheet even though they drive for only 3 hours on each day of the week:
(a) True
(b) False

200. When an employee-driver keeping 'domestic' records changes jobs, to whom must they return their record book?
(a) the Traffic Commissioner
(b) they must keep it themselves for at least 12 months
(c) their new employer
(d) the employer who issued it

201. Written records need not be kept by drivers engaged on British domestic operations who, on any day, do not drive for more than 4 hours and who do not drive outside a radius from the vehicle operating centre of:
(a) 30 miles
(b) 35 kilometres
(c) 50 kilometres
(d) 50 miles

202. A driver must retain their completed domestic record book for at least:
(a) 2 days
(b) 7 days
(c) 14 days
(d) 1 month

203. Drivers using weekly record books under the domestic rules must return them to their employer for examination and signature within:
(a) 5 days
(b) 7 days
(c) 10 days
(d) 14 days

204. Employers are required to keep completed record books and duplicate daily record sheets for at least:
(a) 6 months
(b) 9 months
(c) 12 months
(d) 15 months

205. For which of the following vehicles does EU law require drivers to make statutory records of their hours of work?
(a) those not exceeding 3.5 tonnes gross plated weight
(b) those exceeding 3.5 tonnes permissible maximum weight
(c) those under 1,525 kg unladen weight
(d) all vehicles except those of the fire, police and military services

206. Which of the following officials has legal authority to inspect a goods vehicle driver's records of hours of work:
(a) a traffic warden
(b) a public health inspector
(c) a Customs officer
(d) a police officer in uniform

207. A VOSA examiner or a uniformed police officer may enter premises to inspect drivers' and vehicle records:
(a) at any time with the owner's permission
(b) at any reasonable time
(c) only during working hours
(d) after giving 48 hours' notice

208. Police have statutory powers to enter premises to inspect drivers' records:
(a) only between 9.00 am and 5.00 pm
(b) at any reasonable time
(c) at any time with the owner's consent
(d) they have no such powers

209. An enforcement officer may legally demand the production of tachograph records at a specified Traffic Area office within a period of:
(a) 3 days
(b) 5 days
(c) 7 days
(d) 10 days

210. Which of the following penalties could be imposed on a vehicle operator by a Traffic Commissioner for contravention of the drivers' hours rules?
(a) up to six months' imprisonment
(b) a fine of up to £250
(c) endorsement of their ordinary licence
(d) revocation, suspension or curtailment of the 'O' licence

211. Which of the following countries is a signatory to the AETR agreement?
(a) Estonia
(b) Poland
(c) Hungary
(d) Bulgaria

212. How many hours can be driven in the current week by a driver operating under the EU drivers' hours rules (3820/85/EEC) who drove for 56 hours during the previous week?
(a) 48 hours
(b) 56 hours
(c) 34 hours
(d) 45 hours

213. Under the AETR drivers' hours rules the daily driving limit of 9 hours may be extended to 10 hours:
(a) under no circumstances
(b) on one occasion in a week
(c) on two occasions in a week
(d) on three occasions in a week

214. The weekly limit on driving time for a driver of a 38-tonne vehicle on an international journey operating under AETR rules is:
(a) 60 hours
(b) 50 hours
(c) 40 hours
(d) 6 daily driving shifts

215. The driver of a goods vehicle on an international road haulage journey from the UK is restricted by the AETR agreement to a maximum two-weekly driving limit of:
    (a) 56 hours
    (b) 64 hours
    (c) 82 hours
    (d) 90 hours

216. On an international journey, in which of the following countries would a UK driver of an over-3.5-tonne vehicle be subject to the AETR drivers' hours rules?
    (a) Hungary
    (b) Poland
    (c) Slovakia
    (d) Romania

217. Drivers operating under AETR rules must take a minimum weekly rest period of:
    (a) 22 hours
    (b) 29 hours immediately preceded or followed by a daily rest period
    (c) 45 hours
    (d) 45 hours immediately preceded or followed by a daily rest period

TACHOGRAPHS

218. Where a driver drives more than one goods vehicle during their day's work, they must complete one tachograph chart:
    (a) for each vehicle driven that day
    (b) for the vehicle driven for the longest period in the day
    (c) for the first vehicle driven that day
    (d) if practicable, to cover all the vehicles driven in the day

219. When completing a daily tachograph chart the driver should:
    (a) record the exact time at which any vehicle changeover took place
    (b) record the time of changeover to the nearest 15 minutes
    (c) record the time of changeover to the nearest 30 minutes
    (d) record just the relevant vehicle registration numbers

220. A motor fitter driving a vehicle which falls within Regulation 3821/85/EEC on a local road test after repair must complete a tachograph chart:
    (a) True
    (b) False

221. When commencing a day's work an LGV driver must enter which of the following information in the centre field of their tachograph chart?
    (a) the time at which they commenced the shift
    (b) the name and address of their employer
    (c) the place from which they commenced their day's journey
    (d) the amount of daily rest taken prior to commencing the shift

222. If a tachograph chart is damaged while in use by the driver:
    (a) it must be attached to the chart used to replace it
    (b) it must be retained by the driver for at least 21 days
    (c) it can be destroyed or retained by the driver as they wish
    (d) it must be returned to the employer as soon as is reasonably possible

223. A tachograph instrument must be installed so that when opened, but without removing the chart, the recordings can be read for the previous:
    (a) 6 hours
    (b) 8 hours
    (c) 9 hours
    (d) 10 hours

224. A broad black trace made on a tachograph chart indicates that:
    (a) the vehicle is moving
    (b) the engine is running while the vehicle is standing
    (c) the tachograph face is not properly closed
    (d) the driver has turned the mode switch to record driving

225. With a two-man tachograph, the chart for the non-driving crew member will show recordings of:
    (a) distance and activity mode only
    (b) speed and distance only
    (c) speed, activity mode, distance and time
    (d) activity mode and time only

226. Drivers are required to keep tachograph charts with them, and available for inspection by the enforcement authorities, for:
    (a) the current week only
    (b) the current week plus the previous week
    (c) the current week plus the last day of the previous driving week
    (d) the current week plus the last 2 days of the previous week

227. Completed tachograph charts must be returned to the employer no later than:
    (a) 7 days after use
    (b) 12 days after use
    (c) 14 days after use
    (d) 21 days after use

228. Tachograph charts must be retained by the operator and kept available for inspection, if required, by the enforcement authorities for at least:
    (a) 12 months
    (b) 15 months
    (c) 21 months
    (d) 24 months

229. A driver who is unavoidably delayed on a journey and has exceeded the EU drivers' hours limits must:
    (a) notify the Traffic Area office with details as soon as possible
    (b) report the facts to the police as soon as possible
    (c) enter the details on their tachograph chart for that day
    (d) report the circumstances to an enforcement officer within 24 hours

230. Under EU Regulations, a calibrated tachograph installation must be fitted to which of the following vehicles?
    (a) a goods vehicle with a permissible maximum weight of 3.5 tonnes used only in the UK
    (b) a local-authority refuse-collection vehicle with a permissible maximum weight of 10 tonnes
    (c) a delivery vehicle with a permissible maximum weight of 2 tonnes used only in national road transport operations
    (d) a goods vehicle with a permissible maximum weight of over 3.5 tonnes used for national and international journeys

231. When presenting an articulated vehicle to an approved tachograph centre for tachograph calibration, only the tractive unit is needed for this purpose:
    (a) True
    (b) False

232. When a newly installed tachograph is first calibrated the vehicle must be:
    (a) unladen
    (b) fully loaded
    (c) loaded above 3.5 tonnes gross weight
    (d) standing on a gradient of less than 16 per cent

233. Responsibility for ensuring that the tachograph installed in a vehicle functions correctly at all times rests with:
    (a) the driver only
    (b) the vehicle operator only
    (c) both the driver and the operator
    (d) the vehicle owner

234. The law requires tachographs to be re-calibrated at approved centres in the United Kingdom every:
    (a) 1 year
    (b) 2 years
    (c) 3 years
    (d) 6 years

235. The speed recording mechanism in a tachograph must be accurate 'in use' to within:
    (a) plus or minus 6 kilometres per hour at speeds in excess of 10 kph
    (b) plus or minus 6 kilometres per hour at all speeds
    (c) 10 per cent at speeds above 10 mph
    (d) plus or minus 10 per cent at all speeds

236. A new 'plaque' must be fitted to the tachograph after re-calibration every:
    (a) 6 years
    (b) 3 years
    (c) 2 years
    (d) 1 year

237. Tachograph 'checks' must be carried out by an approved fitter or workshop every:
    (a) 5 years
    (b) 4 years
    (c) 3 years
    (d) 2 years

238. Responsibility for ensuring that seals on the connections between the tachograph head and the gearbox remain intact on a goods vehicle rests with:
    (a) the vehicle operator only
    (b) the driver only
    (c) both the operator and the driver
    (d) the installation fitter or workshop

239. If a tachograph becomes unserviceable during a journey, it must be repaired en route if the vehicle is unable to return to base within a maximum of:
    (a) 2 days
    (b) 2 weeks
    (c) 1 week
    (d) 10 days

240. When travelling on international journeys a British driver must ensure that their tachograph always shows the official time in the UK:
    (a) True
    (b) False

241. An EU-approved tachograph used in a goods vehicle on an international journey from Reading to Madrid must:
    (a) be switched off when the driver is taking a statutory break
    (b) be kept operating only while the vehicle is travelling on the road but not during the cross-channel ferry crossing
    (c) be kept operating continuously from the time the driver takes over the vehicle until he or she returns to base
    (d) be operated only while the driver is at the wheel of the vehicle

242. If a tachograph breaks down on an international journey it must be repaired en route if, counting from the day of the breakdown, the vehicle is unable to return to base within:
    (a) 2 days
    (b) 3 days
    (c) 5 days
    (d) 7 days

243. When driving under EU drivers' hours rules on an international journey the driver must have with them, and be able to produce, their tachograph charts for:
    (a) the previous 2 weeks
    (b) the previous 7 days
    (c) the current week and their last driving day in the previous week
    (d) all driving since their last international journey

CHAPTER 7

Typical questions: Fiscal law

(covering syllabus sections D1, D2, D3 and D4)

VALUE ADDED TAX (VAT)

244. The threshold at which VAT registration becomes legally necessary is based on:
    (a) weekly profitability
    (b) annual taxable turnover
    (c) the type of business operated
    (d) the previous year's tax demand

245. A taxable person is one who:
    (a) is registered or liable to register for VAT
    (b) pays income tax in instalments
    (c) pays National Insurance contributions
    (d) must register for corporation tax

246. The amount of VAT added to sales invoices by a haulier is called:
    (a) input tax
    (b) sales tax
    (c) purchase tax
    (d) output tax

VEHICLE EXCISE DUTY (VED)

247. The minimum period for which a vehicle excise licence may be obtained is:
(a) 3 months
(b) 6 months
(c) 9 months
(d) 12 months

248. As a general rule, vehicle excise duty for heavy goods vehicles is payable according to:
(a) their unladen weight
(b) whether they are rigid or articulated
(c) their gross weight and the number of axles
(d) the number of axles

249. Where vehicle excise duty is originally paid for 12 months but is no longer required after 9 months, application for a refund of duty for each complete month remaining on the licence may be made:
(a) True
(b) False

250. Which of the following classes of vehicle is not exempt from excise duty?
(a) veterinary ambulances
(b) farmers' goods vehicles
(c) fire service vehicles
(d) vehicles en route to a place by prior appointment for annual test

251. If a vehicle owner is convicted of keeping a vehicle on the road without a current excise licence in force, they may be fined and ordered to pay back duty for the period during which the vehicle was unlicensed:
(a) True
(b) False

252. A goods vehicle with an unladen weight of 1,550 kg is liable for excise duty based on:
(a) its gross plated weight
(b) its unladen weight
(c) the private/light goods (PLG) duty rate
(d) the number of axles

253. Vehicle excise duty payable for an articulated goods vehicle combination with a gross train weight of 12,000 kg is based on:
   (a) the unladen weight and the number of axles
   (b) its gross train weight only
   (c) its gross train weight and the number of axles on the tractive unit
   (d) its gross train weight and the total number of axles

254. Excise duty is chargeable in respect of goods-carrying trailers in which of the following circumstances?
   (a) where the trailer exceeds 4 tonnes gross weight and is towed by a vehicle exceeding 12 tonnes gross weight
   (b) where the trailer exceeds 2 tonnes gross weight and is towed by a vehicle exceeding 12 tonnes gross weight
   (c) where the trailer exceeds 2 tonnes gross weight and is towed by a vehicle not exceeding 12 tonnes gross weight
   (d) where the trailer exceeds 1 tonne gross weight and is towed by a vehicle exceeding 4 tonnes gross weight

255. A goods vehicle with an unladen weight of 1,625 kg will be subject to excise duty on the basis of:
   (a) its gross plated weight
   (b) the PLG rate
   (c) its unladen weight
   (d) the rigid goods vehicle rate

256. Additional excise duty payable when a rigid goods vehicle draws a trailer exceeding 4,000 kg gross weight applies when the gross weight of the towing vehicle exceeds:
   (a) 1,525 kg
   (b) 7,500 kg
   (c) 12,000 kg
   (d) 16,260 kg

257. For which of the following vehicle combinations may excise duty be paid for operation at a gross train weight of 40 tonnes:
   (a) a tractive unit with 3 axles and a semi-trailer with 1 axle
   (b) a tractive unit with 3 axles and a semi-trailer with 2 axles
   (c) a tractive unit with 2 axles and a semi-trailer with 1 axle
   (d) a tractive unit with 2 axles and a semi-trailer with 2 axles

258. If an operator leaves a broken-down vehicle with an expired excise licence parked on the road, they are:
    (a) not liable to be prosecuted because no offence was committed
    (b) liable to prosecution because they have committed the offence of being the keeper of an unlicensed vehicle on the road
    (c) not liable to prosecution because the vehicle was there only temporarily due to the breakdown
    (d) not liable to prosecution if they can prove it was genuinely broken-down

259. The law requires the display of a vehicle excise licence disc:
    (a) in the windscreen where it can easily be seen
    (b) in the windscreen on the nearside
    (c) in the windscreen or a nearside window
    (d) in a window to the front of the driver's seat

260. If Customs and Excise officers wish to examine a goods vehicle their principal concern will be to ensure that:
    (a) the correct amount of vehicle excise duty has been paid
    (b) the operator is registered for VAT and makes proper returns
    (c) the fuel in the tank is duty-paid diesel, not gas oil
    (d) the driver is carrying a proper record of the weight of the load

TRADE LICENCES

261. The maximum period for which a trade licence may be taken out is:
    (a) 6 months
    (b) 12 months
    (c) 2 years
    (d) 4 years

262. Application for a trade licence has to be made to:
    (a) the Department of Trade and Industry
    (b) the Driver and Vehicle Licensing Agency
    (c) a Local Vehicle Registration Office
    (d) a local office of HM Customs and Excise

263. The maximum number of trade licences permitted for a transport operator carrying out vehicle servicing and maintenance is:
    (a) 1
    (b) 2
    (c) 4
    (d) not restricted

264. On the grant of a trade licence a pair of trade plates is issued for attachment to vehicles used under the licence. The plate containing the triangular licence must be:
(a) displayed on the front of the vehicle
(b) displayed at the rear of the vehicle
(c) displayed in the windscreen
(d) attached so as to cover the existing registration plate

265. Trade plates issued under a trade licence are made up with:
(a) black letters and numbers on a red background
(b) black letters and numbers on a white background
(c) red letters and numbers on a black background
(d) red letters and numbers on a white background

266. A trade licence issued for use on vehicles:
(a) must be attached to the trade plate carried at the rear of the vehicle
(b) must be attached to the trade plate carried at the front of the vehicle
(c) must be displayed in the windscreen of the vehicle in use
(d) need not be displayed provided the plates are attached to the vehicle

267. If a trade licence is refused an appeal can be made in writing within 28 days to:
(a) the Local Vehicle Registration Office
(b) a magistrate's court
(c) the Secretary of State for Transport
(d) the head of the Driver and Vehicle Licensing Agency

268. Which of the following activities would constitute legal use of a trade licence?
(a) to permit temporary use of a vehicle with an expired excise licence
(b) a haulier road-testing their unlicensed vehicle after repair
(c) to allow a perishable load to be transferred to an untaxed vehicle following a breakdown
(d) to enable a person publicizing a new vehicle to drive it before it is licensed

269. A vehicle being operated under a trade licence:
    (a) must not be used for the carriage of goods
    (b) may carry a load when necessary to demonstrate the capabilities of the vehicle
    (c) may carry a load provided it belongs to the trade licence holder
    (d) may carry a load but only between points specified in the licence

270. A service vehicle used by a haulier for towing broken-down vehicles and collecting vehicle components may be used under a trade licence:
    (a) True
    (b) False

271. Which passengers may be legally carried on a vehicle operated under a trade licence?
    (a) a person in a broken-down vehicle being towed
    (b) a prospective customer assessing the capabilities of the vehicle
    (c) a friend of the licence-holder being given a lift home
    (d) an employee of the licence-holder being given a lift home

272. In what circumstances would the holder of a trade licence be acting unlawfully?
    (a) by using it on a recovery vehicle
    (b) by failing to display a current 'O' licence disc on a goods vehicle in addition to the trade plates
    (c) by using a vehicle under the licence to carry goods for demonstration purposes
    (d) by allowing the vehicle to remain parked on a public road when not in use

273. Which of the following uses is not permitted under the terms of a trade licence?
    (a) delivering a load while road-testing a vehicle following annual test preparation
    (b) collecting a new vehicle from the bodybuilder
    (c) demonstrating a vehicle to a prospective purchaser
    (d) collecting components for the vehicle from the supplier

ROAD AND BRIDGE TOLLS

274. Road tolling is a scheme usually devised to:
    (a) raise revenue for health and safety projects
    (b) raise revenue to fund new road building and to control congestion
    (c) stop vehicles using roads and tunnels
    (d) increase usage of secondary routes

275. In the UK, the Queen Elizabeth II Bridge:
    (a) forms the boundary between Devon and Cornwall
    (b) links the Scottish mainland to the Isle of Skye
    (c) links the M8, M9 and M90 motorways west of Edinburgh
    (d) runs parallel to the Dartford Tunnel

276. Switzerland imposes a road tax on vehicles in transit through its territory based on:
    (a) gross weight and the length of stay in the country
    (b) payload tonnage and the distance travelled in the country
    (c) kilometres travelled within the country
    (d) a tonnage rate for the amount of payload

277. At the frontier of which of the following countries is a kilometre tax payable on vehicles based on their gross weight and the distance travelled?
    (a) Greece
    (b) Croatia
    (c) Portugal
    (d) Sweden

278. Which of the following countries imposes a road user charge for vehicles with a maximum payload capacity of over 12 tonnes entering its territory?
    (a) Denmark
    (b) Austria
    (c) Germany
    (d) Republic of Ireland

279. France sets a limit on the amount of fuel that can be imported in the fuel tanks of a goods vehicle when entering its territory before excise duty is payable:
    (a) True
    (b) False

280. The maximum amount of road fuel in normal tanks that can be imported duty-free in a vehicle entering Germany is:
    (a) 50 litres
    (b) 100 litres
    (c) 200 litres
    (d) unspecified

281. Before additional duties become payable, the amount of road fuel that can be imported in vehicle running tanks according to an EU Directive is:
    (a) 50 litres
    (b) 100 litres
    (c) 200 litres
    (d) 250 litres

CORPORATE AND INCOME TAX

282. Corporation tax is levied on:
    (a) local authorities
    (b) passenger transport operations
    (c) the profits of limited and public liability companies
    (d) the shareholders of public companies

283. Income tax is payable by:
    (a) all companies
    (b) employed individuals and self-employed traders
    (c) shareholders of companies
    (d) limited liability companies

284. Income tax is deducted from the wages of employees under a system known as:
    (a) PAYE
    (b) self-assessment
    (c) tax deduction
    (d) DETR

285. For tax purposes a self-employed person is legally required to produce only:
    (a) a balance sheet
    (b) their VAT returns
    (c) a statement of their income and all expenditure
    (d) a statement of income (accounting for business expenses is voluntary)

286. The law requires that tax records must be kept for at least:
    (a) five years from 31 January in the year following the tax year
    (b) three years from the end of the tax year
    (c) six years from the end of the tax year
    (d) twelve years from the beginning of the tax year

287. Corporation tax for large companies is currently set at a rate of:
    (a) 50 per cent of turnover
    (b) 30 per cent of gross profit
    (c) 25 per cent of net profit
    (d) 45 per cent of annual turnover

288. Double taxation relief means:
    (a) relief from future taxes due to overpayment in a previous year
    (b) relief from tax due to an error by the Inland Revenue
    (c) allowing foreign tax paid as a credit against UK tax liability
    (d) exemption from paying tax in certain years due to extenuating circumstances

289. A double tax treaty applies where:
    (a) the UK has agreed with another country that tax should not be charged in both countries
    (b) an individual lives in the UK and works abroad and the law requires tax to be paid in two countries
    (c) a person has both a full-time and a part-time job both providing taxable earnings
    (d) a limited company is liable to tax under its corporate name and trading name

290. A self-employed owner–driver is required to pay:
    (a) Class 1 national insurance contributions
    (b) Class 3 national insurance contributions
    (c) Class 2 national insurance contributions only
    (d) Class 2 contributions and Class 4 contributions subject to profits earned

CHAPTER 8

Typical questions: Business and financial management
(covering syllabus sections E1 to E13)

PAYMENT METHODS

291. How does a firm of 'factors' provide a company with funds?
    (a) by acting as a debt collection agency
    (b) by buying a company's fixed assets and leasing them back
    (c) by purchasing debts to the company for immediate cash
    (d) by reducing the time limits given to customers in which to pay

292. Where a firm with an inadequate cash flow sells its invoices at less than their face value to a third party, this is called:
    (a) provision for bad debts
    (b) trade invoicing
    (c) debt factoring
    (d) debt collection

293. The term 'carriage forward' means that payment for the carriage of goods:
    (a) has already been made by the consignor
    (b) will be made by the consignee
    (c) will be made later by the consignor
    (d) will be made by the consignor's forwarding agent

294. One method by which a road-haulage operator can encourage customers to pay their accounts more promptly is to:
(a) offer them a trade discount
(b) offer them a cash discount
(c) permit them to pay by credit transfer
(d) permit them to pay in cash instead of by cheque

295. Which of the following constitutes a 'credit sale'?
(a) payment by cheque
(b) payment by Visa/MasterCard
(c) payment by giro cheque
(d) payment by postal order

296. Credit transfer is a method of payment for goods or services:
(a) by crossed cheque
(b) using a bank cheque card
(c) using Visa/MasterCard or other credit card
(d) direct into the creditor's bank account

297. A haulier may demand payment in advance for the carriage of
goods:
(a) only after the goods have been delivered to the customer
(b) only within a limited period before he receives the goods
(c) only when the goods are received by him for delivery
(d) as soon as the contract is entered into

298. Which of the following defines a 'cash sale'?
(a) where immediate payment in full is made
(b) where payment is made in cash
(c) where payment is by either cheque or cash
(d) payment where a receipt rather than an invoice is required

299. When a budget-account credit arrangement is agreed, whereby
goods may be purchased up to so many times a regular monthly
repayment, who actually makes the loan?
(a) a finance company
(b) a bank
(c) the retailer
(d) a credit card organization

300. If a purchaser fails to pay for goods or services within a stipulated
period, the vendor may charge interest on the money owed:
(a) under no circumstances whatever
(b) under any circumstances if they believe the purchaser will pay

    (c) providing the purchaser is notified in writing that interest will be charged within 30 days of the account becoming due for payment

    (d) providing the purchaser was notified of the fact in writing at the time the purchase was made

301. A footnote on an invoice that payment terms are '2.5 per cent one month' means that the recipient:

    (a) will have to pay 2.5 per cent interest per month for each month the account remains unpaid

    (b) may deduct 2.5 per cent from the total amount owing if payment is made within one month

    (c) must pay at least 2.5 per cent of the total amount due within one month

    (d) must pay the total amount of the account less 2.5 per cent within one month

CREDIT AND BORROWING

302. A shopper wishing to buy goods but not to have to pay for them until some weeks later would use a:

    (a) hire-purchase agreement

    (b) debit card

    (c) membership card

    (d) credit card

303. Taking credit or loans has a number of advantages, but it has the following particular disadvantage:

    (a) it gives delayed access to goods

    (b) it provides goods at higher prices

    (c) it involves payment of interest

    (d) it inhibits cash discounts

SOURCES OF FUNDS

304. Which of the following is an internal source of company funds?

    (a) reducing investment in stock

    (b) offering preference shares to employees

    (c) obtaining a bank overdraft

    (d) making a share scrip issue

305. The high-street clearing banks offer which of the following types of funds?
    (a) long-term capital investment
    (b) debentures
    (c) investment opportunities
    (d) short-term financing facilities

306. Which of the following is a source of short-term financing for a typical road haulier?
    (a) a debenture issue
    (b) an issue of ordinary shares
    (c) retained profits of the company
    (d) a bank overdraft

307. What is the main advantage of using hire purchase as a source of funds?
    (a) the firm never owns the goods, so does not have a devaluing asset
    (b) the length of loan period is usually long and interest rates are low
    (c) essential equipment can be acquired with minimum capital outlay
    (d) equipment acquired this way can readily be disposed of if it becomes redundant

308. A firm needing to employ additional labour for a short-term contract entailing an additional outlay of some £30,000 would most readily raise the extra funds:
    (a) by seeking a bank overdraft
    (b) by making a rights share issue
    (c) by an additional share issue
    (d) by raising a debenture

309. Which would be the best way of financing increased stocks of raw materials?
    (a) by hire-purchase loan
    (b) by leasing stock
    (c) by reducing the credit given to customers
    (d) by bank overdraft facility

310. Debentures issued as a source of funds would be described as:
    (a) long-term loans
    (b) ordinary share stock
    (c) preference share stock
    (d) retained profits

311. Debentures carrying a mortgage on the firm's premises would appear in its balance sheet under the general heading of:
    (a) current liabilities
    (b) long-term liabilities
    (c) ordinary shares
    (d) share capital

312. The long-term funds of a company would normally include:
    (a) its bank overdraft
    (b) its petty-cash float
    (c) the value of its debtor invoices
    (d) the original capital invested when the company was started

313. A source of short-term funds for a business would be:
    (a) a mortgage on premises
    (b) the firm's share capital
    (c) a bank overdraft facility
    (d) capital invested by the founders of the firm

314. Ordinary shares issued by a limited company are considered to be:
    (a) a source of long-term funds
    (b) a source of short-term funds
    (c) a long-term asset
    (d) a short-term liability

315. Which of the following would be treated as short-term company funds?
    (a) its ordinary shares
    (b) its tax reserves
    (c) its debenture stock
    (d) the capital employed

316. Limited liability companies must pay debenture holders annual interest on their loans:
    (a) only if they can afford to do so
    (b) even if trading losses have been made during the year
    (c) if the shareholders agree that such interest should be paid
    (d) on a voluntary basis but only if profits have been made

317. Which of the following financial measures would not assist in raising funds for a business?
    (a) an issue of preference shares
    (b) a rights issue of ordinary shares
    (c) raising a debenture
    (d) a shareholder selling their shares

BALANCE SHEETS AND ASSETS

318. A balance sheet is a statement of company affairs at a given date showing:
    (a) its annual sales and purchases
    (b) its operating costs
    (c) its detailed operating expenditure
    (d) its assets and liabilities

319. A company balance sheet is a statement of its financial position:
    (a) for the 13 four-weekly trading periods
    (b) for the financial year
    (c) for any fixed period
    (d) at a given date

320. The Companies Act requires a limited company to produce a balance sheet every:
    (a) 6 months
    (b) 9 months
    (c) 12 months
    (d) 24 months

321. Which company official is required to certify that the balance sheet of a company gives a true and accurate statement of the company's financial affairs?
    (a) the Registrar of Companies
    (b) its officially appointed auditors
    (c) one or all of the directors
    (d) the company secretary

322. The amount of a firm's capital may be determined by examining:
    (a) its trading account
    (b) its annual balance sheet
    (c) its profit-and-loss account
    (d) its management accounts

323. Stocks of vehicle and heating fuel would be shown in a firm's balance sheet as:
    (a) fixed assets
    (b) current assets
    (c) current liabilities
    (d) long-term liabilities

324. Which of the following would be shown as current assets in a company balance sheet?
 (a) amounts owing to creditors
 (b) its current overdraft and any bank loans
 (c) credit balances in its bank accounts and petty cash in hand
 (d) dividends to be paid to shareholders

325. A debenture is shown in a company's balance sheet as:
 (a) a current liability
 (b) a long-term liability
 (c) a fixed asset
 (d) a current asset

PROFIT-AND-LOSS ACCOUNT

326. Which of the following would not be shown in a firm's profit-and-loss account?
 (a) tax paid in the year
 (b) the total amount of capital employed in the business
 (c) annual depreciation on its fixed assets
 (d) interest on any bank or other loans

327. Which of the following would appear in a firm's trading and profit-and-loss account?
 (a) its total annual turnover
 (b) amounts owing to creditors
 (c) its bank overdraft at the year end
 (d) the value of its unpaid debtors

328. Which of the following would be a direct expense on a firm's profit-and-loss account?
 (a) local authority rates on premises
 (b) anticipated benefits from advertising
 (c) a vehicle repair contract
 (d) additional share allocations

329. A financial statement of annual sales turnover, expenditure and net profit for a firm over a given period is called:
 (a) an income and expenditure report
 (b) a trading and profit-and-loss account
 (c) the balance sheet
 (d) a management account

330. A company's annual trading and profit-and-loss account shows:
    (a) the assets of the company and its liabilities
    (b) payments received and expenditure incurred
    (c) the current market value of the company's vehicles and fixed assets
    (d) the value of its debtor and creditor accounts

331. From the following figures, which appear in the balance sheet of XY Haulage Limited, determine the amount of total capital employed.

	£		£
Share Capital	140,000	Property	110,000
Debentures	20,000	Motor vehicles	36,000
Creditors	24,000	Debtors	36,000
Bank overdraft	6,000	Cash reserves	8,000
	190,000		190,000

    (a) £140,000
    (b) £160,000
    (c) £166,000
    (d) £190,000

332. Which of the companies below has the highest rate of return on capital employed?

	Company A £	Company B £	Company C £	Company D £
Issued Share Capital	100,000	200,000	300,000	400,000
Net Profit	20,000	30,000	40,000	50,000

    (a) company A
    (b) company B
    (c) company C
    (d) company D

333. What is the percentage rate of return on total capital employed for a firm which produces a balance sheet showing the following figures?

	£
Issued Share Capital	175,000
Bank overdraft	25,000
Gross Profit	40,000
Net Profit	25,000

   (a) 12.5 per cent
   (b) 15 per cent
   (c) 20 per cent
   (d) 25 per cent

334. The total capital employed in a business can be established by taking:
   (a) its fixed assets plus its current assets
   (b) its current liabilities plus its current assets
   (c) its fixed assets minus its current assets
   (d) its fixed and current assets minus its current liabilities

335. A business is said to be under-capitalized if it suffers from:
   (a) too few paid-up shareholders
   (b) a low value of fixed assets compared to current assets
   (c) insufficient low-interest loans
   (d) too low a ratio of current assets to current liabilities

336. A creditor would appear in a firm's balance sheet as:
   (a) a fixed asset
   (b) a current asset
   (c) part of its share capital
   (d) a current liability

337. Money owed to a business by its customers is shown in its balance sheet under:
   (a) fixed assets
   (b) creditors
   (c) debtors
   (d) unpaid loans

PROFITABILITY AND FINANCIAL RATIOS

338. Which of the following financial calculations will show the net worth of a company?
    (a) the value of its assets plus its liabilities
    (b) the value of its assets multiplied by its liabilities
    (c) the value of its assets less its liabilities
    (d) the value of its assets divided by its liabilities

339. Which ratio can be calculated from a firm's annual profit-and-loss account?
    (a) annual turnover as a percentage of total capital employed
    (b) gross profit as a percentage of annual turnover
    (c) fixed capital as a percentage of total capital employed
    (d) current ratio

340. If a firm's final accounts show profit as £25,000 on an annual turnover of £200,000, what is its profit margin?
    (a) 10.0 per cent
    (b) 12.5 per cent
    (c) 13.5 per cent
    (d) 20.0 per cent

341. Which of the following figures is needed to calculate return on capital employed?
    (a) net profit
    (b) gross profit
    (c) current assets
    (d) current liabilities

342. The figure representing the total capital employed in a business is the total of its issued share capital and reserves, plus any:
    (a) credit balance at the bank and cash in hand
    (b) long-term loans
    (c) unpaid debtors
    (d) current assets

343. A company's fixed and current assets less the value of its current liabilities represents its:
    (a) net worth
    (b) working capital
    (c) trading profit
    (d) total capital employed

344. A company's return on capital can be established from which of the following ratios?
(a) net profit divided by capital employed
(b) current assets divided by current liabilities
(c) total annual sales divided by total capital employed
(d) annual turnover divided by total sales

345. Which of the following accounting terms describes the working capital of a business?
(a) the value of plant, machinery and vehicles
(b) the ordinary share capital of the business
(c) petty cash in hand plus credit balances at the bank
(d) current assets less current liabilities

346. Which of the following operating expenses is debited against a firm's working capital?
(a) payment for diesel fuel
(b) capital invested in new workshop equipment
(c) the purchase of new and replacement vehicles
(d) the acquisition of a new office computer

347. Which of the following items would be described as a current liability?
(a) a bank overdraft
(b) the value of stocks held
(c) the amount of a firm's debtors
(d) the contents of a petty-cash float

348. The working-capital ratio of a business can be established by comparing:
(a) its creditors to debtors
(b) its net profit to the total capital employed
(c) its excess of current assets over current liabilities
(d) its petty-cash float to the bank overdraft

349. What is a firm's working-capital ratio if its current assets are £40,000 and its current liabilities are £20,000?
(a) 1:1
(b) 1:2
(c) 2:1
(d) 5:1

350. If a company's annual accounts show a profit, allowing for corporation tax, of £45,000 and the value of net assets as £180,000, its return on net assets will be:
    (a) 2.5 per cent
    (b) 12.5 per cent
    (c) 25 per cent
    (d) 45 per cent

351. Which financial ratio can be calculated from the trading and profit-and-loss account?
    (a) total capital employed as a percentage of annual turnover
    (b) current ratio
    (c) gross profit as a percentage of annual turnover
    (d) liquidity ratio

352. A firm with liquid assets of £315,000, a stock holding worth £220,000 and current liabilities of £150,000 has an acid-test ratio of:
    (a) 0.5:1
    (b) 1.2:1
    (c) 1.5:1
    (d) 2.1:1

353. The usual formula for calculating current ratio is:
    (a) liquid working capital divided by current liabilities
    (b) current assets divided by current liabilities
    (c) annual net profit divided by total capital employed
    (d) bad debts divided by the value of current assets

354. Which of the following current ratios calculated from a company balance sheet would be considered the most favourable?
    (a) 0.25:1
    (b) 0.5:1
    (c) 1:1
    (d) 2:1

355. With current assets of £1,000,000 and current liabilities of £500,000 a firm has a current ratio of:
    (a) 2:1
    (b) 2.5:1
    (c) 3:1
    (d) 4:1

356. If a company's annual accounts show current assets of £75,600 and current liabilities of £36,000 its current ratio will be:
    (a) 1:1
    (b) 1:2
    (c) 2:1
    (d) 2.1:1

357. A firm's liquid assets divided by its current liabilities represents a statement of:
    (a) its liquidity ratio
    (b) its current ratio
    (c) its interest cover
    (d) its debtor/creditor ratio

358. A firm with a liquidity ratio of 0.5:1 would:
    (a) be in a healthy position
    (b) have a high level of sales
    (c) suffer from cash-flow problems
    (d) be technically insolvent

359. A company with annual accounts showing liquid assets of £60,000 and current liabilities of £85,000 has a liquidity ratio of:
    (a) 1:1
    (b) 0.6:1
    (c) 0.85:1
    (d) 0.7:1

360. A creditor of a company is a person or firm:
    (a) who owes the company money
    (b) who grants credit to the company
    (c) to whom the company grants credit
    (d) to whom the company owes money

361. If a person purchased 1,000 items at £20 each and sold 900 of them at £25 each, their gross profit from the sales would be:
    (a) £2,500
    (b) £5,000
    (c) £18,000
    (d) £22,500

CASH FLOW

362. Which of the following can be used as a measure of 'cash flow' in business?
    (a) cash received less debts owing to the business
    (b) funds received and cash paid out by the business
    (c) cash flowing out of the business to meet day-to-day commitments
    (d) net profits made by the business

363. Firms usually overcome their short-term cash-flow problems by:
    (a) an issue of debenture stock
    (b) an issue of redeemable preference shares
    (c) arranging overdraft facilities with their bank
    (d) offering increased trade discounts to customers

364. When a firm is experiencing cash-flow difficulties, one way of overcoming this is to:
    (a) make an effort to increase sales
    (b) give customers longer periods of credit
    (c) factor its sales invoices
    (d) increase productivity by overtime working

365. Which of the following financial policies would improve a firm's cash flow?
    (a) paying creditors promptly
    (b) paying all accounts on receipt of purchase invoice
    (c) purchasing early while prices are stable
    (d) reducing the periods of credit given to debtors

366. A haulier could improve their cash-flow position by:
    (a) obtaining extended credit from suppliers
    (b) allowing debtors longer periods to pay their accounts
    (c) paying creditors more promptly
    (d) purchasing new vehicles

367. A 'cash budget' could be defined as:
    (a) a record of cash received by a business
    (b) a record of the cash expenditure of a business
    (c) a plan for ensuring future sales
    (d) a plan for future cash income and expenditure

368. A business needing to assess its likely cash position six months ahead should prepare:
    (a) a half-yearly profit-and-loss account
    (b) a review of last year's trading performance
    (c) a cash-flow forecast
    (d) an updated balance sheet

369. In haulage, as in any other business, if possible, foreseeable purchases should:
    (a) be planned for action when cash outflow is at a peak
    (b) be planned for action when cash inflow is at a peak
    (c) be planned for action when cash inflow is at a low level
    (d) not be planned for the future but actioned as soon as required

370. A cash-flow statement would be prepared by a firm to indicate:
    (a) the inflows of cash from its trading activities
    (b) how its cash resources have been utilized over a given period
    (c) its cash balances at the end of the period
    (d) the sources and uses of funds over a given period

DEBTORS AND LIQUIDATION

371. A firm's debtors are those:
    (a) who owe it money for work/supplies invoiced
    (b) to whom it owes money
    (c) from whom it has obtained loans
    (d) taking legal action against it for non-payment of debts

372. On default of payment of its debts, a firm's creditors may apply to a court for it to be compulsorily 'wound up':
    (a) True
    (b) False

373. If a company has been voluntarily 'wound up', the liquidator is released from their duty:
    (a) on authorization from the Official Receiver
    (b) on authorization from the Registrar of Companies
    (c) on application by the creditors to the Department of Trade and Industry
    (d) by a resolution of both shareholders and creditors at the final creditors' meeting

BUDGETS

374. A budget is:
    (a) a financial plan for the future
    (b) an estimate of available cash
    (c) a type of operating schedule
    (d) a form of vehicle costing

COSTS AND DEPRECIATION

375. If a vehicle has fixed charges of £10,000 per year and covers 40,000 miles at a running cost of 25p per mile, what gross profit will be made if it is hired out at 60p per mile?
    (a) 5 pence per mile
    (b) 10 pence per mile
    (c) 15 pence per mile
    (d) 20 pence per mile

376. If a vehicle has 80 litres of fuel in its tank at the start of a journey and after covering 90 kilometres it has 50 litres left, the average fuel consumption will be:
    (a) 2.0 km/litre
    (b) 2.66 km/litre
    (c) 3.0 km/litre
    (d) 3.33 km/litre

377. Which of the following is not usually a direct objective of vehicle-costing activities?
    (a) calculating drivers' wage rates
    (b) calculating haulage rates
    (c) planning efficient distribution operations
    (d) planning capital investment programmes

378. Direct costs in haulage operations are defined as:
    (a) the general administrative costs of a business
    (b) the overhead costs of a haulage business
    (c) costs that have been previously incorporated in the budget
    (d) costs that can be directly attributed to vehicle operations

379. Which of the following would be a direct operating cost on a haulage business?
    (a) advertising and publicity to attract new business
    (b) the provision of directors' and management business cars
    (c) local authority annual rates on haulage premises
    (d) replacement tyres

380. When analysing goods vehicle costs, which of the following items would be identified as indirect costs?
(a) quarterly telephone accounts
(b) drivers' wages
(c) vehicle excise duty
(d) vehicle repairs and maintenance

381. An operator should be able to differentiate between the fixed and variable or running costs for vehicles. Which of the following is a fixed cost?
(a) unscheduled vehicle repairs
(b) regular inspection and servicing of vehicles
(c) local authority rates
(d) drivers' overnight accommodation on away journeys

382. A vehicle with total standing costs of £12,000 per year costs 20p per mile to run over 30,000 miles annually. To make 20 per cent gross profit, the charge-out rate would need to be:
(a) 60p per mile
(b) 65p per mile
(c) 72p per mile
(d) 75p per mile

383. In a business, the direct costs are those that:
(a) are met directly from petty cash
(b) are paid immediately by cheque from the bank account
(c) relate directly to the administration of the business
(d) are directly attributable to a cost centre

384. A vehicle which is hired out at 60p per mile has fixed costs of £10,000 per year and costs 25p per mile over 40,000 miles annual running. What is the gross profit margin?
(a) 10 per cent
(b) 12 per cent
(c) 15 per cent
(d) 20 per cent

385. By increasing the miles run by a vehicle, the total cost per mile will:
(a) reduce
(b) increase
(c) remain the same
(d) multiply by the daily distance covered

386. Weekly standing costs for a goods vehicle are £350 and the running cost is 35p per mile. If the vehicle covers 1,000 miles per week, the operating cost per week is:
    (a) £70
    (b) £700
    (c) £100
    (d) £1,000

387. Costs that increase as the miles run by a vehicle increase are called:
    (a) on-costs
    (b) marginal costs
    (c) variable costs
    (d) establishment costs

388. An operator employs part-time drivers to operate an occasional service with a vehicle that would otherwise be idle. The extra drivers' wages would be treated as:
    (a) an indirect cost
    (b) a marginal cost
    (c) an on-cost
    (d) a fixed cost

389. Vehicle running costs are usually determined on a basis of:
    (a) cost per kilometre
    (b) tonne/km
    (c) fixed costs
    (d) establishment costs

390. Which of the following items is identified as a running cost?
    (a) training of staff
    (b) advertising haulage services
    (c) entertaining business customers
    (d) vehicle fuel supplies

391. Which of the following would be classified as a vehicle variable cost?
    (a) maintenance of depot premises
    (b) maintenance of vehicles
    (c) depreciation of vehicles
    (d) insurance of vehicles

392. Which of the following costs is usually mileage based?
    (a) staff and management salaries
    (b) vehicle excise licences
    (c) depreciation charges
    (d) fuel and lubricating oil

393. What is the tyre cost per mile if a set of new tyres for a vehicle, excluding the spare, costs £1,500 and their anticipated life is 45,000 miles?
    (a) 2.66p per mile
    (b) 3.00p per mile
    (c) 3.33p per mile
    (d) 3.66p per mile

394. If a set of tyres for a vehicle costs £1,000 and has a life of 50,000 miles the cost per mile will be:
    (a) 1p
    (b) 2p
    (c) 2.5p
    (d) 3p

395. In quoting for a haulage contract, which of the following items would be calculated as vehicle running costs?
    (a) fuel only
    (b) drivers' wages only
    (c) both drivers' wages and holiday pay
    (d) vehicle depreciation, tax and insurance

396. Which of the following items is a fixed vehicle cost?
    (a) tyres
    (b) vehicle insurance
    (c) maintenance costs
    (d) drivers' night-out expenses

397. Which of the following would be classed as standing costs in a haulage business?
    (a) vehicle excise licences
    (b) office staff salaries
    (c) tyres
    (d) bulk supplies of fuel and lubricants

398. In vehicle costing which of the following is usually classed as a standing cost?
    (a) maintenance and repairs to vehicles
    (b) life insurance on key employees
    (c) vehicle depreciation
    (d) fuel and oil supplies

399. It is important for hauliers to be able to distinguish between the fixed and variable costs in their operations. Which of the following items is a fixed cost?
    (a) vehicle breakdown repairs
    (b) premises insurance
    (c) regular vehicle safety inspections
    (d) drivers' night-out expenses

400. In vehicle-costing calculations, which of the following items would be included in the total standing costs for vehicles?
    (a) depreciation, fuel and tyres
    (b) vehicle servicing, lubricants, interest on capital
    (c) vehicle insurance, drivers' bonus payments and fleet maintenance
    (d) excise licences, vehicle insurance and drivers' basic wages

401. Which of the following would be regarded as a fixed expense in costing vehicle operations?
    (a) fuel
    (b) tyres
    (c) servicing and repairs
    (d) insurance premiums

402. Telephone charges incurred by a haulage company are classed as:
    (a) running costs
    (b) standing costs
    (c) indirect costs
    (d) direct costs

403. Which element of drivers' wages could be considered a fixed cost?
    (a) the basic wage
    (b) overtime payments
    (c) productivity bonuses
    (d) meal and night-out expenses

404. When calculating haulage rates, which of the following would be a standing cost?
    (a) vehicle insurance
    (b) drivers' away-from-home expenses
    (c) tyres
    (d) diesel fuel

405. Although a goods vehicle may not be in use, it still incurs:
(a) running costs
(b) standing costs
(c) overhead costs
(d) marginal costs

406. A haulier looking to achieve 30 per cent gross profit on a vehicle for which the annual fixed costs are £9,000 and the running costs are 25p per mile for 45,000 miles per year would need to charge:
(a) 50p per mile
(b) 55p per mile
(c) 58.5p per mile
(d) 60p per mile

407. The term 'depreciation' used in vehicle costing is most simply defined as:
(a) the value of a vehicle at the end of its useful life
(b) the average value of a vehicle over its anticipated life
(c) the resale value of a vehicle at any point during its useful life
(d) a financial allowance to account for the deterioration of a vehicle throughout its life due mainly to wear and tear

408. The financial act of 'writing off' the value of an asset over its anticipated life is called:
(a) residual valuation
(b) depreciation
(c) revaluation
(d) appreciation

409. Inclusion of a provision for the depreciation of vehicles when compiling a haulage rate quotation would be under the heading of:
(a) standing costs
(b) variable costs
(c) overhead costs
(d) indirect costs

410. Some people prefer to calculate vehicle depreciation as a variable cost based on miles run, but normally this is only justified:
(a) when a vehicle runs very high annual mileages
(b) when hire charges are calculated on a miles run basis
(c) when a vehicle is let out on contract hire
(d) when a vehicle covers only very low annual mileages

411. During a period of high inflation it would be more prudent for a haulier to calculate the depreciation of vehicles on the basis of:
(a) current value
(b) original purchase price
(c) estimated new price
(d) replacement cost

412. An operator buys a lorry for £14,000 and estimates its resale value after six years to be £1,250; the original set of tyres cost £750. What amount must the operator set aside per annum by way of depreciation using the straight-line method?
(a) £1,500
(b) £2,000
(c) £2,200
(d) £2,500

413. An operator purchases a vehicle for £15,000 and then depreciates it using the reducing-balance method at a fixed 20 per cent per annum, thus setting a resale-value target at the end of two years of:
(a) £8,500
(b) £9,600
(c) £10,750
(d) £11,800

414. A vehicle costing £10,000 is estimated to have a useful life of five years and a residual value of £1,000. By the straight-line method, the annual allowance for depreciation would be calculated as:
(a) £800
(b) £1,800
(c) £2,200
(d) £2,800

415. Using the straight-line method of calculation on a £16,000 vehicle with an anticipated life of six years and a residual value of £4,000, the annual depreciation charge would be:
(a) £1,500
(b) £2,000
(c) £2,500
(d) £3,000

416. Using the reducing-balance method of calculation on a vehicle costing £15,000 with an anticipated life of five years and a 25 per cent write-down, the first-year depreciation charge would be:
    (a) £2,750
    (b) £3,750
    (c) £4,750
    (d) £5,750

417. A new vehicle costing £69,500, with six wheels fitted with tyres worth £250 each, is written down by the straight-line method to £12,000 over seven years, resulting in an annual depreciation charge of:
    (a) £6,800
    (b) £7,800
    (c) £8,000
    (d) £9,800

418. If a vehicle purchased for £62,000 has a residual value of £6,000 after an estimated life of seven years, by the straight-line method of calculation the annual rate of depreciation would be:
    (a) £6,200
    (b) £7,500
    (c) £8,000
    (d) £8,500

419. A new vehicle costing £61,500 has six wheels with tyres worth £250 each. Calculating depreciation by the reducing balance method at 25 per cent per annum, the value after two years would be:
    (a) £33,750
    (b) £23,750
    (c) £19,750
    (d) £36,750

420. By the reducing-balance method of calculating depreciation for a vehicle costing £50,000 with an anticipated life of five years and a depreciation rate of 20 per cent per annum, the annual depreciation charge for the first year would be:
    (a) £5,000
    (b) £10,000
    (c) £15,000
    (d) £20,000

421. In a haulage operation, which of the following items would be included under the heading of overhead costs of the business?
(a) the transport manager's salary
(b) vehicle excise licences
(c) drivers' basic wages
(b) lubricating oils

422. The general administrative costs of running a haulage business would be classed as:
(a) marginal costs
(b) variable costs
(c) overhead costs
(d) standing costs

423. The overhead costs of a road haulage business would include:
(a) vehicle insurance
(b) employer's share of pension contributions
(c) interest on capital
(d) vehicle maintenance

424. In assessing the costs of running a haulage business, overheads are those which:
(a) are directly attributable to the vehicles
(b) cover the general administrative costs of the business
(c) arise directly from the ownership of the vehicles
(d) arise after vehicle fixed and variable costs have been recovered

425. Which of the following is an establishment charge on a haulage business?
(a) drivers' wages
(b) office stationery
(c) drivers' night-out expenses
(d) vehicle breakdown costs

426. If a haulage firm's costs are made up as follows, what is the total of its overhead costs?

General administrative costs	£30,000
Management salaries	£50,000
Vehicle maintenance, fuel and tyres	£150,000
Annual depreciation charges	£70,000
Drivers' wages	£90,000

(a) £50,000
(b) £80,000
(c) £150,000
(d) £310,000

427. A haulage fleet comprises five vehicles having the following carrying capacities: two vehicles of 5 tonnes each, two vehicles of 10
tonnes each and one vehicle of 20 tonnes. If the annual overhead
costs, which amount to £15,000, are allocated to each of the vehicles
on the basis of payload capacity, each of the 10-tonners would bear:
(a) £1,500
(b) £2,500
(c) £3,000
(d) £3,500

428. A five-vehicle fleet covers the following average annual distance:
two vehicles average 60,000 km each, two vehicles average 90,000
km each and one vehicle averages 150,000 km. If the firm's overhead
costs, which total £13,500 annually, are allocated to the vehicles on
a per kilometre basis, a vehicle averaging 50,000 km per annum
would carry an annual cost of:
(a) £500
(b) £1,000
(c) £1,500
(d) £2,500

ORGANIZATION

429. An organization is a:
(a) type of computer virus
(b) group of people working together to achieve a common goal
(c) name for a limited company
(d) small fleet of specialized vehicles

430. A firm would prepare an organization chart to show:
(a) the hierarchy of management and staff
(b) when accounts are due for payment
(c) when vehicles are due for service and annual test
(d) when insurance premiums are due for payment

431. Work plans are used by firms to:
    (a) determine when vehicles and trailers are due for MOT testing
    (b) show the Inland Revenue that proper tax records are being kept
    (c) ensure that proper insurance cover applies to vehicles on CMR work
    (d) set out the individual tasks to be carried out to complete a project

MARKETING

432. Market research can be conducted in a number of different ways. When this activity is confined to examining internal documentation, newspapers, trade journals and suchlike, it is generally called:
    (a) local research
    (b) internal research
    (c) desk research
    (d) document research

433. Marketing can be categorized into a number of different spheres. Where a firm gives away pens, hats and T-shirts showing its name and logo, this is generally called:
    (a) advertising
    (b) public relations
    (c) market research
    (d) sales promotion

434. Where a haulage firm makes a special effort to give a good impression to its neighbours and other local people, this is called:
    (a) sales promotion
    (b) public relations
    (c) community publicity
    (d) local advertising

435. A haulier booking a slot on local radio would allocate the cost to their:
    (a) operations budget
    (b) advertising budget
    (c) petty cash
    (d) current account

436. A specialist bulk-liquid haulier would benefit from an advertising spot on national TV:
    (a) True
    (b) False

437. A haulier sending out mailing letters to which potential customers are asked to reply would be doing:
 (a) direct-response advertising
 (b) customer sampling
 (c) sales promotion
 (d) public relations

INSURANCE

438. Besides third-party motor insurance, against which of the following additional risks must a haulier legally have insurance cover?
 (a) passenger liability
 (b) accidental damage to their own vehicles
 (c) loss by fire
 (d) theft from their own vehicles

439. A road haulier is required by law to have which of the following insurance cover?
 (a) goods-in-transit
 (b) fire
 (c) employers' liability
 (d) fidelity guarantee

440. A driver's mate, carried on a haulage vehicle in the course of his work, would be covered for personal injury under the terms of his firm's:
 (a) consequential-loss insurance
 (b) third-party insurance
 (c) fidelity-guarantee insurance
 (d) employers' liability insurance

441. Compulsory employers' liability insurance is intended to cover claims:
 (a) by customers injured by using defective products
 (b) by employees alleging unfair dismissal
 (c) by employees injured at work
 (d) for loss of production due to industrial action

442. A road haulier wishing to cover against loss of trade in the event of a fire at their premises would take out which of the following types of policy?
 (a) consequential loss
 (b) loss-by-fire
 (c) public liability
 (d) employers' liability

443. A haulier wishing to insure against liability for death or injury to a third party as a result of the defective loading of one of their vehicles would take out a policy covering:
    (a) consequential loss
    (b) public liability
    (c) third-party risks
    (d) employers' liability

444. A haulage vehicle loaded with empty drums is being driven on a road when one of the drums falls off, causing damage to a following vehicle. What type of insurance would cover the driver's employer for the damage to the following vehicle?
    (a) goods-in-transit
    (b) employers' liability
    (c) fidelity guarantee
    (d) public liability

445. Loss of company property due to an employee's fraudulent actions is normally covered by which of the following insurances?
    (a) employers' liability
    (b) fidelity guarantee
    (c) consequential loss
    (d) third-party risks

446. A person sustains injury while visiting a haulier's premises. What type of insurance would cover the haulier against the claim for damages?
    (a) consequential loss
    (b) fidelity guarantee
    (c) employers' liability
    (d) public liability

447. Which type of insurance covers against loss of goods carried on a vehicle?
    (a) theft
    (b) goods-in-transit
    (c) employers' liability
    (d) motor vehicle

448. Which of the following types of insurance would provide cover against loss of property as a result of thieves gaining entry to premises?
    (a) public-liability cover
    (b) endowment insurance

(c) all-risks insurance

(d) third-party motor cover

449. The 'excess clause' in a goods-in-transit insurance policy means that:

(a) goods held for an excessive period are no longer covered

(b) the operator is responsible for paying the first part of each claim

(c) goods carried for an excessive distance are not covered

(d) claims in excess of a certain value are not covered

450. An 'immobilizer' clause in a goods-in-transit insurance policy means that the vehicle:

(a) must not be left unattended on a road at night

(b) must be fitted with an approved anti-theft device

(c) must only be parked in approved parks overnight

(d) is not to carry goods during the hours of darkness

451. A restrictive 'night-risk' clause contained in a goods-in-transit policy means that:

(a) goods must be transported only during the hours of daylight

(b) goods will be covered against the additional risks of night transport

(c) vehicles must not be left unattended at night unless fitted with approved anti-theft devices

(d) goods of very high value must not be transported at night unless special insurance cover is obtained

452. The legal requirement for compulsory third-party vehicle insurance is set out in:

(a) the Road Vehicles (Construction and Use) Regulations 1986

(b) the Highways Act 1980

(c) the Road Traffic Offenders Act 1988

(d) the Road Traffic Act 1988

453. Which of the following motor vehicles are exempt from the requirement for compulsory third-party insurance cover?

(a) goods vehicles being operated under a trade licence

(b) vehicles operated by a county or district council in England or Wales

(c) vehicles travelling to or from a place to be tested

(d) vehicles operated by a person who is non-resident in the UK

454. An insurance company offering motor insurance in compliance with legal requirements must be:
    (a) a member of a Lloyds insurance syndicate
    (b) a member of the Motor Insurers' Bureau
    (c) approved by the Department of Trade and Industry
    (d) approved by the Insurance Ombudsman

455. To avoid any resulting liabilities, a passenger can legally agree with the driver to travel in a vehicle entirely at the passenger's own risk:
    (a) True
    (b) False

456. Insurance cover provided by a certificate of motor insurance becomes valid:
    (a) 24 hours after the certificate has been issued
    (b) when the certificate is in the post to the insured
    (c) only when the insured has the certificate in their possession
    (d) from the time the insured telephones vehicle details to the insurers

457. A certificate of motor insurance must contain details of:
    (a) the persons authorized to drive vehicles covered by the policy
    (b) the premiums paid on the policy
    (c) whether excise duty has been paid on vehicles covered by the policy
    (d) whether the vehicles covered are the subject of a hire-purchase agreement

458. The legal requirement for the vehicle owner to pay for emergency hospital treatment for persons injured in a road-traffic accident involving their vehicle would be covered by their:
    (a) fidelity-guarantee insurance
    (b) consequential-loss insurance
    (c) third-party motor insurance
    (d) employer's liability insurance

459. For which of the following offences could a goods vehicle operator be held liable although not driving the vehicle concerned at the time the offence was committed?
    (a) failure to hold third-party insurance cover for the vehicle
    (b) failure to stop following a road accident
    (c) failure to comply with traffic directions
    (d) failure to give particulars at the scene of an accident

460. If a driver cannot produce a certificate of insurance when requested to do so by a police officer, it must be produced at a police station:
(a) personally within 24 hours
(b) personally within 3 days
(c) personally within 5 days
(d) personally or by somebody on their behalf within 7 days

461. If a vehicle not covered by third-party insurance knocks down a pedestrian, a lamp-post and a garden wall, who can successfully claim compensation under the Motor Insurers' Bureau scheme?
(a) the pedestrian only
(b) the owner of the lamp-post
(c) the owner of the garden wall
(d) the pedestrian, and the owners of the lamp-post and the garden wall

462. If an employee driver is charged with driving a vehicle while not insured against third-party risks, they have a valid defence if they can prove the vehicle was not theirs and they had no reason to believe it was not insured:
(a) True
(b) False

463. In addition to third-party motor insurance, for which of the following is a vehicle operator required by law to have insurance cover?
(a) passenger liability
(b) damage to their own vehicles
(c) fire
(d) theft of their own vehicles

464. As an alternative to normal third-party cover taken out with an insurance company a vehicle owner may deposit a sum of money as security with:
(a) the Supreme Court
(b) the Secretary of State for Transport
(c) a Chief Constable of police
(d) the Home Office

465. An organization wishing to carry its own third-party motor insurance risks may do so, provided it deposits with the Accountant General of the Supreme Court as security the sum of:
(a) £15,000
(b) £50,000
(c) £500,000
(d) £5,000,000

466. The insurance Green Card is a compulsory requirement for transiting EU states:
    (a) True
    (b) False

467. Carrying an insurance Green Card means that:
    (a) the driver does not have to surrender their documents to the police following an accident
    (b) the insurance covers more than the basic minimum requirements in EU countries
    (c) the driver will not be held by the police following a road accident
    (d) any fines imposed by police abroad will be covered

ELECTRONIC DATA AND DATA PROTECTION

468. EDI is an acronym for the system used to:
    (a) pass commercial data by electronic means
    (b) play electronic games on computers
    (c) measure energy consumption in industry
    (d) control Ease of Dynamic Intelligence

469. E-commerce is a term used to describe:
    (a) an easy way of shopping in supermarkets
    (b) energy consumption in commercial offices
    (c) conduct of commerce and retail business via the Internet
    (d) electronic learning of foreign languages

470. The Data Protection Act 1998 prohibits:
    (a) firms from keeping any addresses on computer files
    (b) individuals from writing to firms whose addresses they have obtained via computer
    (c) the exchange of data about commercial activities
    (d) the disclosure of information about living and identifiable persons

471. Intelligent Transport Systems are used to:
    (a) provide jobs for people with IT degrees
    (b) provide on-line transport and traffic information and control systems
    (c) keep track of foreign vehicles operating illegally in the UK
    (d) monitor aircraft safety systems

COMMERCIAL TRANSACTIONS

472. In commercial transactions which of the following would constitute an order?
(a) a price list of charges for business services
(b) a request from a supplier for payment of money owed
(c) a form detailing goods consigned for delivery by public carrier
(d) a request by a customer to be supplied with goods or services

473. For which of the following purposes is an advice note used?
(a) to advise customers that goods are about to be delivered
(b) to advise customers that goods ordered are out of stock
(c) to advise a transport department to make a delivery
(d) to advise customers that quoted prices are subject to change

474. Which of the following documents would be used regularly by a haulier?
(a) a consignment note
(b) a bill of lading
(c) a cover note
(d) a debit note

475. The document carried on a vehicle showing delivery addresses, the number of consignments to be delivered and with a space for the consignee to sign as having received the goods is known as:
(a) an invoice
(b) a waybill
(c) a consignment note
(d) a bill of lading

476. A haulier considering the repair of a badly damaged vehicle asks a garage about the likely cost. The garage will initially provide:
(a) an invoice for the work
(b) an order for the job
(c) a statement of the cost
(d) an estimate of labour, time and materials

477. A firm requested to specify the cost of its services and to state whether credit terms are available does so by means of:
(a) an invoice
(b) a statement
(c) a credit note
(d) a quotation

478. A quotation is a formal notification, usually in writing:
    (a) from a supplier to a customer, stating the amount owed for work done
    (b) from a customer requesting the supply of goods or services
    (c) from a supplier reminding a customer how their account stands
    (d) to a customer, giving a specific price for a particular job

479. Due to a clerical error in preparing an invoice, a haulier undercharges a customer for work done. The haulier would correct this by:
    (a) sending the customer a statement of account
    (b) sending the customer a debit note
    (c) making necessary alterations on the invoice
    (d) issuing the customer with a credit note

480. When might a purchaser request a credit note in their favour?
    (a) if damaged goods have been returned to them
    (b) if they return damaged goods to the supplier
    (c) to ensure prompt payment of their account
    (d) to ensure the vendor pays their account promptly

481. The document issued in business to correct an overcharge on an invoice is called:
    (a) a tender
    (b) a debit note
    (c) a statement
    (d) a credit note

482. In which of the following circumstances might a credit note be issued?
    (a) when charges for goods supplied are omitted from an invoice
    (b) when a customer is due for a refund
    (c) when goods were undercharged on the invoice
    (d) to show a customer how their account stands

483. A haulier would send customers a request for payment for work done by means of:
    (a) a debit note
    (b) a proof-of-delivery note
    (c) an invoice
    (d) a statement

484. A statement of account is a commercial document:
    (a) used for invoicing export consignments
    (b) reminding a customer how their account stands with the supplier
    (c) notifying customers of the price for carrying out a job
    (d) sent by a purchaser confirming acceptance of the price charged

485. Which of the following is the correct use of the term 'account rendered'?
    (a) for goods and services invoiced and paid for
    (b) for goods and services paid for but not yet supplied
    (c) for goods and services invoiced
    (d) for goods and services for which the account has been returned as incorrect

486. Statements of account are sent to customers to:
    (a) show their total indebtedness to the supplier at a particular date
    (b) show the credit limit allowed by the supplier
    (c) show the amounts charged by the supplier for goods or services
    (d) charge for additional expenses unknown when the original invoice was raised

487. Which of the following details do not normally appear on a statement of account?
    (a) adjustments for debit and credit notes issued
    (b) discounts available to the customer for prompt payment
    (c) totals of the invoices issued during the period
    (d) descriptions of the goods or services supplied

488. A customer denies receiving certain goods although proof exists that the goods were delivered, so they are sent a copy of the document they signed when receiving them. A copy of which commercial document would be sent?
    (a) the consignment note relating to the delivery
    (b) the advice note notifying delivery
    (c) the invoice for the job
    (d) the order form requesting delivery

489. Which of the following bank accounts would a haulier open to lodge day-to-day cheque receipts and issue cheques to pay business expenses?
    (a) a savings account
    (b) a current account
    (c) a deposit account
    (d) a budget account

490. To ensure a cheque can be paid only into a named bank account it should be:
    (a) left open
    (b) clearly crossed with two heavy lines
    (c) crossed with the words '& Co' between the crossing lines
    (d) crossed with the words 'a/c payee' between the crossing lines

491. A bank account that allows use of the cheque system is called:
    (a) a high-interest deposit account
    (b) a Giro account
    (c) a current account
    (d) a deposit account

492. The main advantage to the recipient of a 'banker's draft' is that:
    (a) it can be converted into cash
    (b) the bank on which it is drawn must honour it when it is presented
    (c) it does not have to be cashed through a bank account
    (d) interest will be paid on it if it is not cashed within six months

493. In a cheque transaction, which of the following is the payee of the cheque?
    (a) the bank on which the cheque is drawn
    (b) the individual on whose account the cheque is drawn
    (c) the person or firm to whom payment is to be made
    (d) the individual who pays in the cheque to the bank

494. Cheques are normally honoured by the banks only if they are presented within:
    (a) 3 months
    (b) 6 months
    (c) 9 months
    (d) 12 months

495. A haulage driver who has no bank account asks their employer to pay their wages by a cheque that they can readily change into cash. The employer would need to give them:
    (a) a crossed cheque
    (b) a cheque crossed ' & Co'
    (c) a cheque crossed 'a/c payee'
    (d) an open cheque

496. A returned cheque marked 'Refer to drawer' means there are insufficient funds in the account of the drawer to cover the amount shown:
    (a) True
    (b) False

497. With the direct-debit system of regular payments from a bank account, it is a disadvantage to the debtor because:
    (a) their creditors have access to details of their bank account
    (b) payments do not take account of monthly fluctuations
    (c) they do not always know the amount debited to their account
    (d) they cannot delay payment of an account

498. Credit transfer is a means of paying for goods or services:
    (a) by computerized invoicing
    (b) using MasterCard, Visa or a similar type of credit card
    (c) direct into the creditor's bank account
    (d) using a bankers' cheque card

499. When a firm decides to pay suppliers' accounts direct through its bank rather than by issuing cheques, it would set up a system known as:
    (a) deferred credit
    (b) direct debit
    (c) standing order
    (d) credit transfer

500. Which of the following statements describes payment of a 'bearer' cheque at a bank?
    (a) only the named payee may cash it but it must be endorsed
    (b) the person presenting it can only have it paid into an account
    (c) only the named payee may cash it
    (d) anyone presenting it to the bank on which it is drawn may receive cash for it

501. Why is it important to keep file copies of purchase orders?
    (a) to check against the invoice when the goods are received
    (b) to avoid pilferage of stock
    (c) to ensure suppliers do not make short deliveries
    (d) for checking stock movements

502. When fluctuating exchange rates result in the French franc being raised in relation to sterling, expenses for a British haulier in France will be:
    (a) lower
    (b) the same
    (c) higher

503. If France devalues the franc by 10 per cent, this will result in:
    (a) reduced costs for UK hauliers in France
    (b) increased costs for UK hauliers in France
    (c) unchanged costs for UK hauliers in France

504. If the French franc is weak in relation to sterling, a UK driver buying fuel in France would:
    (a) find the cost to be less in sterling
    (b) find the cost to be more in sterling
    (c) notice no difference in costs between France and the UK
    (d) be better advised to pay for the fuel in francs

STOCK CONTROL

505. Buying for stock can be justified for which of the following reasons?
    (a) items will be on hand, avoiding delays until supplies arrive
    (b) capital tied up in stocks cannot be diverted to other uses
    (c) surplus stock can be always sold off later
    (d) obsolete stock can be 'written-off' for tax purposes

506. Which of the following stocks would be classed as obsolete?
    (a) stock for which demand is slow and irregular
    (b) stock which is in high seasonal demand
    (c) stock purchased in readiness for changing demand
    (d) parts for equipment replaced by new and updated versions

507. Effective stock control in a heavy-vehicle workshop will:
    (a) result in accumulation of excessive stocks
    (b) reduce the amount of capital reserves tied up in stock
    (c) jeopardize the company's cash-flow position
    (d) reduce the financial resources available for more pressing purposes

508. When carrying out a physical check of fuel stocks, the amount on hand should be:
    (a) opening stock – deliveries from the supplier + issues to vehicles
    (b) opening stock + deliveries from the supplier – issues to vehicles
    (c) opening stock + issues to vehicles + deliveries from the supplier
    (d) deliveries from the supplier – issues to vehicles + opening stock

509. On checking its fuel storage tank, a haulage firm found its fuel stock was valued at £1,628. During the accounting period, fuel amounting to £2,785 had been delivered and a check on the previous balance showed an amount carried forward of £843. What was the value of fuel used during the period?
    (a) £1,000
    (b) £1,628
    (c) £2,000
    (d) £2,461

510. A firm's fuel storage tank held 2,603 litres at the start of a period and 27,400 litres of new stock was received. If 26,503 litres were issued how much fuel should now be in the tank?
    (a) 503 litres
    (b) 2,603 litres
    (c) 3,500 litres
    (d) 7,400 litres

FREIGHT AGENTS

511. The system whereby a number of small consignments are consolidated into a unit load is called:
    (a) cabotage
    (b) freight forwarding
    (c) groupage
    (d) containerization

512. Which of the following organizations provides a groupage service?
    (a) a freight forwarder
    (b) the Freight Transport Association
    (c) the Road Haulage Association
    (d) the International Road Transport Union (IRU)

513. In road-haulage operations, a clearing house is:
   (a) an organization which arranges clearance of goods through Customs
   (b) an agency from which hauliers can hire extra drivers and other staff
   (c) a firm which organizes subcontract hauliers to move customers' goods
   (d) the system whereby banks clear each other's cheques

514. A haulier providing a regular service of collecting small consignments, and combining them into bulk loads for transport to destinations where the bulk loads are broken down for local distribution of individual consignments, undertakes the activities of:
   (a) consolidation and break-bulk
   (b) warehousing and distribution
   (c) logistics
   (d) load scheduling

515. An organization set up specifically to organize the movement of loads by the use of subcontracted hauliers is known as:
   (a) a third-part operator
   (b) a contract haulier
   (c) a transport clearing house
   (d) a distribution contractor

516. The consolidation of individual consignments into bulk unit loads to be trunked to a common destination is known as:
   (a) logistics management
   (b) load scheduling
   (c) groupage
   (d) contract distribution

517. In road transport, firms operating as clearing houses provide a service:
   (a) arranging to clear vehicle prohibition notices
   (b) clearing surplus and bankruptcy stocks by organizing bargain sales
   (c) arranging to move loads by subcontracting to small hauliers
   (d) arranging insurance, documentation and Customs clearance of transport documents

518. In road-haulage operations, a firm which arranges with consignors to have their loads transported by subcontract hauliers is called:
    (a) a public carrier
    (b) a national carrier
    (c) a contract haulier
    (d) a clearing house

519. Which of the following organizations provides a 'groupage' service?
    (a) the Road Haulage Association
    (b) the British Institute of Freight Forwarders
    (c) the National Association of Warehouse Keepers
    (d) a freight forwarder

520. A principal haulier can pass liability claims for lost or damaged loads to the subcontractors who transported them:
    (a) True
    (b) False

521. In haulage industry terms, a 'subcontractor' is defined as:
    (a) an agent who undertakes subcontracted commissions for a principal
    (b) a haulage contractor who subcontracts work to other hauliers
    (c) a haulier who undertakes work on behalf of the original contractor
    (d) a forwarding agent who arranges transport and prepares the necessary documentation and insurance

522. In connection with the normal business carried out by firms operating as freight forwarders, which of the following statements is correct?
    (a) export documentation can only be lodged with HM Customs and Excise by an approved freight forwarder
    (b) use of a freight forwarder for customs clearance is not compulsory in the UK
    (c) freight forwarders must hold a certificate of competence before they can offer their services
    (d) freight forwarders should only be used when consigning exports beyond the EU

523. Groupage is a term used to describe the activity:
    (a) where individual consignments are consolidated into a larger single consignment for a trunk haul often by trailer or container
    (b) where transport operators combine to share common premises
    (c) where a freight forwarder integrates deliveries for a group of companies
    (d) where a haulier specializes in combined deliveries to a particular group of countries

524. The function of a transport clearing house is:
    (a) to arrange Customs clearance for vehicles arriving at a port with import or export consignments
    (b) to arrange clearance sales of bankruptcy stocks
    (c) to arrange clearance of vehicles prohibited by DOT examiners
    (d) to arrange for goods to be transported by subcontracted hauliers

525. A haulier offering a regular trailer service for the transport of small consignments to specified destinations where the loads are broken-down for local distribution:
    (a) provides a factoring service
    (b) is a haulage clearing house
    (c) operates a warehousing and distribution service
    (d) provides a groupage service

526. The transportation system whereby a number of small consignments are consolidated into a unit load is called:
    (a) containerization
    (b) groupage
    (c) cabotage
    (d) trunking

527. In haulage terms, if haulier A contracts to carry goods for B, and A in turn subcontracts the work to C and the goods are damaged in transit:
    (a) B should sue A who was the original contractor
    (b) B should sue C who was the subcontractor who carried the goods
    (c) B can sue both A and C since both were party to the movement
    (d) B will rely on A to sue C to recover damages

528. If after a haulier has subcontracted work to another operator the goods are lost in transit the original haulier is:
    (a) fully liable to the customer for the full value of the loss
    (b) not liable to the customer for losses resulting from the action of the subcontractor
    (c) only liable for the loss if the subcontractor fails to compensate the customer
    (d) not liable if they advised the customer that they were subcontracting the work to another haulier

CHAPTER 9

Typical questions: Access to the market

(covering syllabus sections F1 to F5)

OPERATOR LICENSING

529. Operators' licensing in Great Britain is based on the concept of quality control of road transport:
    (a) True
    (b) False

530. Implementation in the UK of EU Directive 561/74 resulted in a change to the pre-existing 'O' licensing scheme by requiring:
    (a) certain transport managers to be professionally competent
    (b) goods vehicle operators to specify suitable parking facilities
    (c) the mandatory introduction of tachographs
    (d) own-account transport operators to hold 'O' licences

531. The Road Traffic Act 1974 added further conditions to 'O' licensing requirements by demanding that licence holders:
    (a) specify a suitable operating centre at which to base their vehicles
    (b) must advertise licence applications in local newspapers
    (c) specify the name of a professionally competent person
    (d) retain vehicle maintenance records for 15 months

532. In connection with operators' licensing, a 'small goods vehicle' is defined as a rigid vehicle with a permissible maximum weight not exceeding:
    (a) 1,525 kg
    (b) 1,750 kg
    (c) 2,040 kg
    (d) 3,500 kg

533. Which of the following vehicles is exempt from 'O' licensing?
    (a) a vehicle constructed to carry goods with a permissible maximum weight of 3 tonnes and drawing a trailer of 2 tonnes gross weight
    (b) a vehicle constructed to carry goods with a permissible maximum weight of 2 tonnes and drawing a trailer of 1,050 kg unladen
    (c) a vehicle constructed to carry goods with a permissible maximum weight of 3.5 tonnes drawing a trailer of 1.5 tonnes gross weight
    (d) a vehicle constructed to carry goods with a permissible maximum weight of 7.4 tonnes

534. A standard 'O' licence is required by the user of a goods vehicle that is:
    (a) over 3.5 tonnes gross weight and used for hire-or-reward haulage
    (b) carrying only the user's 'own goods'
    (c) over 3.5 tonnes for carrying horses for leisure purposes
    (d) used unladen solely for training purposes

535. A basic legal requirement for the grant of an 'O' licence is that the applicant must:
    (a) guarantee to provide services at lower rates than existing hauliers
    (b) comply with the law on drivers' hours and record keeping
    (c) prove need for their services which is not met by other local operators
    (d) not run services which compete with other modes of transport

536. A person wishing to enter the road haulage industry will require a standard national 'O' licence to operate:
    (a) a rigid vehicle of 5 tonnes unladen weight
    (b) a rigid vehicle of 3 tonnes gross plated weight
    (c) an articulated vehicle of 3.5 tonnes gross train weight
    (d) a dual-purpose vehicle and trailer

537. A restricted 'O' licence confines the holder to:
    (a) operations within a radius of 50 km from the operating centre
    (b) operations within a radius of 75 km from the Traffic Area office
    (c) undertake hire-or-reward haulage operations only
    (d) undertake own-account transport operations

538. A manufacturer who plans to operate heavy goods vehicles for distribution of their own goods and occasional loads for customers for hire or reward in the UK and across Europe requires what type of 'O' licence?
    (a) a standard national licence
    (b) a restricted licence
    (c) a restricted international licence
    (d) a standard national and international licence

539. A road haulier applying for an 'O' licence must make:
    (a) separate applications to each Traffic Area in which they have an operating centre
    (b) a consolidated application to the DETR in London
    (c) a single application to only one Traffic Area irrespective of how many operating centres they have
    (d) a single consolidated application to the Transport Tribunal

540. The maximum period for which an operator's licence will be issued in the UK is normally:
    (a) 2 years
    (b) 3 years
    (c) 4 years
    (d) for life unless revoked

541. A company holding a restricted operator's licence is permitted to:
    (a) collect and deliver its own goods within the UK and on the continent
    (b) collect and deliver its own goods, and goods for hire or reward, within the UK and on the continent
    (c) collect and deliver goods for hire or reward or own account but only in the UK
    (d) collect and deliver its own goods in the UK only

542. When a company applies for a restricted operator's licence the Traffic Commissioner will not expect the applicant to:
    (a) arrange to observe the drivers' hours and records regulations
    (b) nominate the name of a person who is professionally qualified
    (c) show they have adequate financial resources
    (d) show that they are a fit and proper person to hold a licence

543. Provided an operator has a current goods vehicle 'O' licence they can operate as many vehicles as they wish:
    (a) True
    (b) False

544. If an operator has two operating centres in one Traffic Area and one operating centre in another, they must hold:
    (a) one operator's licence to cover all the centres
    (b) two operator's licences in one Traffic Area
    (c) three separate operator's licences, one for each centre
    (d) two operator's licences, one in each Traffic Area

545. Windscreen discs issued to a restricted 'O' licence holder are coloured:
    (a) green
    (b) orange
    (c) blue
    (d) yellow

546. In determining the previous conduct of an applicant for an 'O' licence, the Traffic Commissioner will require a declaration of any convictions incurred during the past:
    (a) 3 years
    (b) 5 years
    (c) 7 years
    (d) 10 years

547. When completing the statement of intent on form GV79, the applicant for an 'O' licence is not required to declare that:
    (a) the wages they pay their drivers will comply with Wages Council rates
    (b) they will arrange to ensure that drivers comply with the hours and tachograph law
    (c) vehicle maintenance arrangements will be adequate
    (d) vehicles will not be overloaded

548. The maximum number of 'O' licences that an operator can hold in any one Traffic Area is:
    (a) 1
    (b) 2
    (c) 3
    (d) 4

549. The professional-competence qualification for goods vehicle 'O' licensing can be met:
    (a) collectively by a partnership
    (b) only by an individual person
    (c) by a private limited company
    (d) by the board of directors of a public limited company

550. Full membership of a list of specified professional bodies is one means of meeting the qualification for professional competence but not including:
    (a) the Chartered Institute of Logistics and Transport (CILT)
    (b) the Institute of Road Transport Engineers (IRTE)
    (c) the Institute of Transport Administration (IoTA)
    (d) the Institute of Advanced Motorists

551. When a specified employee transport manager who meets the professional-competence qualification ceases to be of good repute, the 'O' licence will:
    (a) immediately become invalid
    (b) continue in force for 6 months to allow for the appointment of a replacement professionally qualified person
    (c) continue in force for 12 months to allow for the appointment of a replacement professionally qualified person
    (d) continue in force for a 'reasonable period of time' to allow for the appointment of a replacement professionally qualified person

552. If a self-employed standard 'O' licence holder dies or becomes legally incapacitated, the TC can authorize continuation of the licence on the takeover of the business by a new owner for a period of:
    (a) 2 months
    (b) 6 months
    (c) 18 months
    (d) 12 months

553. If 12 months after the death of the designated transport manager an 'O' licence holder has not employed a qualified replacement and as a result the TC takes their licence away, this is defined as:
    (a) a suspension of the licence
    (b) a refusal to grant the licence
    (c) a revocation of the licence
    (d) a curtailment of the licence

554. Under the goods vehicle operators' licensing legislation the term 'financial standing' means:
    (a) the value of the vehicles to be specified on the 'O' licence
    (b) the authorized share capital of the transport business
    (c) the average profitability of the business in previous years
    (d) the availability of sufficient funds to ensure the legal operation of the undertaking

555. Legal requirements for standards of 'good repute' in connection with an application for and the holding of an 'O' licence apply to:
    (a) the licence applicant/holder only
    (b) the operator and all their employees
    (c) both the applicant and the named professionally competent person
    (d) only the nominated professionally competent transport manager

556. 'O' licence holders must advise the TC of any event that affects their good repute, professional competence or financial standing within a period of:
    (a) 7 days
    (b) 14 days
    (c) 28 days
    (d) 2 months

557. The law relating to operators' licensing requires that records of vehicle maintenance must be retained for at least:
    (a) 3 months
    (b) 6 months
    (c) 12 months
    (d) 15 months

558. If an 'O' licence vehicle windscreen disc is lost the licence holder must:
    (a) apply to the Traffic Area for a replacement on form GV79
    (b) apply to the Traffic Area for a replacement on form GV80
    (c) apply to the Traffic Area for a replacement on form GV81
    (d) notify the TC of the loss and a free replacement will be issued

559. When an operator needs to vary their 'O' licence, they should apply to the TC at least:
    (a) 3 weeks in advance
    (b) 4 weeks in advance
    (c) 6 weeks in advance
    (d) 9 weeks in advance

560. The TC must be informed of any changes concerning the legal entity of an 'O' licence holder's business within:
    (a) 7 days
    (b) 14 days
    (c) 28 days
    (d) 2 months

561. For the purposes of goods vehicle 'O' licensing, an 'operating centre' is defined as:
    (a) the place where vehicles are inspected, serviced and repaired
    (b) the licence holder's place of business where vehicle records are kept
    (c) the place where vehicles are kept when not in use
    (d) the registered office of the licence holder's business

562. If an operator parks their vehicles at the premises of a major customer, has them maintained at a commercial garage, and runs the business from their home, officially the 'operating centre' specified on their 'O' licence will be:
    (a) their home
    (b) the driver's home
    (c) the repair garage
    (d) the customer's premises

563. Which of the following bodies has a statutory right to object to the grant of a goods vehicle operator's licence?
    (a) the Road Haulage and Distribution Training Council
    (b) the Health and Safety Executive
    (c) the Road Haulage Association
    (d) the Department for Transport

564. Which of the following organizations can legally object to an application for a goods vehicle 'O' licence?
    (a) the National Association of Warehouse Keepers (NAWK)
    (b) the British Institute of Forwarding Agents (BIFA)
    (c) the British Association of Removers (BAR)
    (d) the Royal Automobile Club (RAC)

565. Which of the following is one of the grounds for a trade union to make a statutory objection to the grant of an operator's licence?
    (a) the applicant has insufficient funds to maintain vehicles
    (b) there is a surplus of unemployed haulage drivers in that area
    (c) the applicant has not set up satisfactory health and safety schemes
    (d) the applicant refuses to recognise a closed-shop agreement

566. Under 'O' licensing regulations an advertisement must be placed in a newspaper circulating in the locality of the proposed operating centre within a period:
(a) not exceeding 21 days before the application is made
(b) from 21 days before to 21 days after the application is made
(c) no later than 21 days after the application is made
(d) of any 42 days before or after the application

567. A person wishing to make an environmental representation against an 'O' licence application following publication of details in a newspaper must send this to the TC within:
(a) 10 days
(b) 21 days
(c) 28 days
(d) 30 days

568. When a statutory objection is made to an application for a goods vehicle 'O' licence the objector must send a copy of their letter to:
(a) the Chief Constable of police
(b) other statutory objectors
(c) the local authority
(d) the applicant at their published address

569. Apart from the list of statutory objectors, which of the following can make an environmental representation against the grant of an 'O' licence?
(a) the National Union of Railwaymen
(b) the local planning authority
(c) the Health and Safety Executive
(d) occupants of neighbouring houses

570. Certain trade unions have a statutory right of objection to the grant of 'O' licences on the grounds that applicants:
(a) have poor industrial relations records
(b) have not set up proper safe-working arrangements
(c) have refused to be party to collective-bargaining agreements
(d) are not persons of good repute

571. An 'O' licence holder who acquires additional vehicles within the number currently authorized on their licence:
(a) should have notified the TC before they acquired the extra vehicles
(b) must notify the TC within 1 month of acquiring them, using form GV80
(c) must notify the TC within 3 months, using form GV80
(d) has no legal need to inform the TC

572. A licence holder who wishes to expand their fleet beyond the total number of vehicles currently authorized on their 'O' licence must:
    (a) apply for an additional licence to cover the extra vehicles
    (b) make a GV81 application to vary their licence
    (c) surrender their existing licence and apply for a new one
    (d) defer the expansion until their current licence expires

573. An operator may transfer a vehicle from one Traffic Area to another in which they hold an 'O' licence without informing the TC, for a period of up to:
    (a) 1 month
    (b) 2 months
    (c) 3 months
    (d) 6 months

574. Under operators' licensing regulations, records of vehicle maintenance must be retained for at least 15 months at:
    (a) the operator's home address
    (b) the place where the vehicles are maintained
    (c) the vehicle operating centre as specified on the 'O' licence
    (d) the operator's registered business address

575. If an 'O' licence application is refused by a Traffic Commissioner the applicant has a right of appeal to:
    (a) the High Court
    (b) the Court of Appeal
    (c) a magistrate's court
    (d) the Transport Tribunal

576. An operator whose 'O' licence is revoked by an LA following convictions for heavy goods vehicle-related offences has a right of appeal to:
    (a) the Transport Tribunal
    (b) the Court of Appeal
    (c) a Crown Court
    (d) the Goods Vehicle Centre, Swansea

577. When an 'O' licence has been suspended or curtailed the TC may direct that the vehicles in question are not to be used under any other 'O' licence for a period:
    (a) not exceeding 3 months
    (b) of a maximum of 6 months
    (c) of up to 9 months
    (d) of no longer than 12 months

578. If an 'O' licence holder is requested to produce their licence at a police station the maximum period which they may be given to do this is:
    (a) 5 days
    (b) 7 days
    (c) 14 days
    (d) 28 days

INTERNATIONAL HAULAGE OPERATIONS

579. A period permit issued under a bilateral agreement permits:
    (a) one return journey only to the country in question
    (b) one return journey within a specified period
    (c) a fixed number of journeys within a specified period
    (d) an unlimited number of journeys during the period of its validity

580. Two types of permit are available under bilateral agreements:
    (a) journey and period permits
    (b) Eco-point and multilateral permits
    (c) EEC and ECMT permits
    (d) piggy-back and road/rail certificates

581. A UK haulage vehicle carrying an international load for delivery in Lisbon via the Dover–Calais cross-channel ferry route would require road haulage permits for:
    (a) France and Spain
    (b) France, Spain and Portugal
    (c) Portugal only
    (d) none of this journey

582. A haulier required by a customer to deliver goods to Turkey would need to apply for a journey permit to the:
    (a) Estonian Embassy in London
    (b) Department of the Environment, Transport and the Regions in London
    (c) Road Haulage Association
    (d) International Road Freight Office

583. A loaded goods vehicle with a permissible laden weight not exceeding 6 tonnes travelling via France on an international journey to Luxembourg would need:
    (a) a French bilateral journey permit
    (b) a Luxembourg bilateral journey permit
    (c) no permit as the operation is within the EU
    (d) an ECMT road haulage permit

584. A driver travels from Dover to Ostend on a cross-channel ferry with a delivery for Ukraine via the Czech Republic and Slovakia. For this journey they would require:
    (a) a road/rail certificate for Germany and Poland
    (b) ECMT road haulage permits for Germany, the Czech Republic and Slovakia
    (c) a Community Authorization and a Ukraine bilateral journey permit
    (d) no permit as the operation is exempt

585. The Goods Vehicles (International Road Haulage Permits) Regulations 1975 make it illegal to undertake a road haulage journey from the UK without a permit to or through:
    (a) the Netherlands and Luxembourg
    (b) Belgium and the Netherlands
    (c) France and Germany
    (d) Turkey

586. The purpose of Community Authorizations issued in the UK is to enable goods vehicles to make international journeys:
    (a) to and from any EU member state
    (b) on return only from another member state
    (c) between 2 EU member states excluding the UK
    (d) between 3 or more member states

587. A UK own-account operator who delivers a load of their own goods to a destination in France under an own-account document is offered a return load from France. What is the legal position?
    (a) they may carry the load if the goods are for use by their own company in the UK
    (b) they may carry the load so long as it does not involve delivery in France
    (c) they may accept the load provided arrangements were made before they left the UK
    (d) they may not accept the return load under any circumstances

588. What type of document would a UK operator need to undertake haulage operations through France, Spain and Portugal?
    (a) a bilateral road-haulage permit
    (b) an EU journey permit
    (c) a Community Authorization
    (d) an EU or ECMT multilateral permit

589. The former system of Cabotage Authorizations allowed a UK haulier to undertake international haulage journeys:
    (a) between the UK and only one other contracting state
    (b) between any number of EU member states
    (c) within the boundaries of any EU member state
    (d) across the whole of the European mainland

590. ECMT road haulage permits are issued to cover road haulage operations between:
    (a) the UK and other EU member states
    (b) the 25 contracting states to the European Conference of Transport Ministers
    (c) the UK and non-EU member states
    (d) the UK and non-members of the ECMT

591. Engagement in EU cabotage operations means the haulier must:
    (a) charge and account for VAT in the country concerned
    (b) give details of their journeys to the Road Haulage Association
    (c) open an international account with Customs and Excise
    (d) take out special cabotage insurance cover

592. When undertaking cabotage journeys a UK haulier must:
    (a) confirm details of all loads to the IRFO
    (b) comply with the rates and conditions of carriage applicable in the country concerned
    (c) return all load-weight tickets to UK Customs and Excise
    (d) advise the RHA of all haulage rates obtained

593. In road haulage terms, cabotage was:
    (a) an illegal act not permitted in any European state
    (b) permitted where valid Cabotage Authorizations had been issued
    (c) illegal only in France, Germany and Italy
    (d) permitted provided a valid ECMT multilateral permit was held

594. Which of the following haulage operations carried out with a UK registered road haulage vehicle would be defined as cabotage?
     (a) collect from Shannon and deliver to Lyon
     (b) collect from Dusseldorf and deliver to Bordeaux
     (c) collect from Rheims and deliver to Montpellier
     (d) collect from Croydon and deliver to Cherbourg

595. If a UK haulier collects and delivers a load between the following European cities, which of the journeys would have been classed as cabotage?
     (a) Rheims and Rotterdam
     (b) Bremerhaven and London
     (c) Brussels and Liege
     (d) Larne and Cork

596. Initial application to the International Road Freight Office for a road haulage permit must be accompanied by which of the following documents?
     (a) a copy of a current CMR insurance certificate
     (b) a copy of the TIR approval certificate for the vehicle/trailer
     (c) the applicant's international 'O' licence
     (d) the applicant's international professional-competence qualification

597. Unless otherwise exempt, the Goods Vehicles (International Road Haulage Permits) Regulations 1975 make it an offence to use a UK vehicle without a valid haulage permit on journeys to or through which of the following countries?
     (a) Austria
     (b) Italy
     (c) Turkey
     (d) Croatia

598. Cabotage Authorizations were valid for:
     (a) 2 weeks
     (b) 1 month
     (c) 3 months
     (d) 6 months

599. A Cabotage Authorization issued by the International Road Freight Office had to be returned by the operator:
     (a) within 7 days after use or, if unused, by the expiry date
     (b) within 15 days after use or, if unused, by the expiry date
     (c) within 30 days after use or, if unused, by the expiry date
     (d) in any case no later than the date of expiry

600. European Union Regulation 4059/89 introduced a system of:
    (a) exemptions for certain road haulage traffic from quotas and permits
    (b) Community Authorizations
    (c) rate tariffs throughout the Union
    (d) Cabotage Authorizations

601. UK hauliers require German third-country permits:
    (a) to undertake international journeys from the UK to Germany
    (b) to carry goods from Germany to countries outside the EU
    (c) to transit Germany to pick up loads from outside the EU
    (d) to authorize unaccompanied trailer operations to Germany

602. The issue of an ECMT permit provides authority to:
    (a) undertake both haulage and own-account operations within the EU
    (b) send unaccompanied trailer traffic to the EU
    (c) undertake international journeys to certain countries outside the EU
    (d) undertake tramping haulage between EU member states

603. Multilateral road haulage permits issued under the auspices of the ECMT are valid for journeys between EU member states and to:
    (a) Bulgaria
    (b) Czech Republic
    (c) Hungary
    (d) Croatia

604. An ECMT removals permit permits the holder to:
    (a) undertake tramping haulage between ECMT contracting states
    (b) operate removals with specialized staff/equipment between ECMT states
    (c) undertake cabotage operations within ECMT contracting states
    (d) carry return loads of furniture from Europe

605. ECMT road haulage permits are valid for haulage operations in:
    (a) EU member states only
    (b) member states of the European Conference of Ministers of Transport
    (c) both EU and Comecon member states
    (d) both EU and EFTA member states

606. Community Authorizations are normally valid for a maximum of:
    (a) six months only
    (b) one year at a time
    (c) three years
    (d) five years

607. Community Authorizations are issued by:
    (a) the TC to international 'O' licence holders
    (b) the DVLC to international 'O' licence holders
    (c) the IRFO to international hauliers who apply
    (d) the EU in Brussels to registered international hauliers

608. When travelling on an international journey the original of the vehicle registration document must be carried on the vehicle:
    (a) True
    (b) False

609. UK vehicles travelling abroad are required to display a national identification plate:
    (a) in all circumstances
    (b) only within the European Union
    (c) only if their gross weight exceeds 3.5 tonnes
    (d) when operating for hire and reward only

610. A person can obtain an international driving permit from the RAC or AA provided they have a current valid driving licence and:
    (a) live in the UK and are at least 18 years of age
    (b) live in the UK and are at least 21 years of age
    (c) can show that there have been no driving convictions in the past year
    (d) are a paid-up member of the AA/RAC/RSAC

611. For undertaking a journey to which of the following countries would it be necessary for a UK driver to have a visa in addition to a passport?
    (a) Portugal
    (b) Azerbaijan
    (c) Croatia
    (d) Hungary

612. To enter which of the following countries would an international haulage driver need to obtain a visa?
    (a) Greece
    (b) Turkey

(c) Belarus
(d) Finland

613. Which of the following countries will still accept a British 'green' driving licence provided that a translation of the licence is also carried?
(a) Italy
(b) Spain
(c) Portugal
(d) Turkey

DOCUMENTS AND ADMINISTRATION

614. What document used in export trade is looked upon as a legal receipt for goods received for shipment or for goods shipped?
(a) a Bill of Lading
(b) a consular invoice
(c) a CMR consignment note
(d) an ATA carnet

615. SITPRO is concerned with:
(a) simplifying documents and procedures in international trade
(b) the quota system for allocating international road haulage permits
(c) the international system for taxation of road vehicles
(d) international Customs procedures for trade within the EU

616. If a hazardous load is to be shipped on a cross-channel ferry, which of the following documents must be presented to the ferry operator?
(a) the CMR consignment note
(b) the bilateral road haulage permit covering the journey
(c) a SITPRO dangerous goods shipping note
(d) an ADR vehicle-approval certificate

617. The SITPRO system provides exporters with:
(a) simplified Customs clearance at national frontiers
(b) automatic pre-entry at Customs offices of departure
(c) aligned documentation
(d) bonds against payment or deposits of Customs duty

618. Single Administrative Documents used as transit documents in conjunction with the Community Transit system must be lodged at the:
    (a) local Customs and Excise office
    (b) office of departure
    (c) office of destination
    (d) International Road Freight Office

619. The acceptance of transit guarantee vouchers when using the full Community Transit system is subject to the approval of the guarantor by the:
    (a) Department of Trade and Industry
    (b) Department of the Environment, Transport and the Regions
    (c) International Road Transport Union (IRU)
    (d) HM Customs and Excise

620. Firms moving goods between the UK and other EU member states can avoid having to lodge individual deposits to cover possible Customs claims if they use:
    (a) authenticated certificates of origin
    (b) Community Transit guarantee vouchers
    (c) CMR consignment notes
    (d) EUR 1-movement certificates

621. A vehicle moving goods from the UK via Italy and overland to Greece must use which of the following Customs systems?
    (a) the Greek national transit system
    (b) Community Transit from the UK through to Greece
    (c) Community Transit to Italy and TIR from Italy to Greece
    (d) TIR for the whole journey

622. Community Transit may be used for international journeys from the EU to which of the following non-EU countries?
    (a) Switzerland
    (b) Bulgaria
    (c) Norway
    (d) Croatia

623. A Community Transit T2 declaration indicates that the goods in question are:
    (a) in free circulation within EU member states
    (b) imported from countries outside the EU
    (c) not in free circulation within EU member states
    (d) in free circulation in Spain and Portugal

624. Community Transit guarantee vouchers are only valid if provided by:
    (a) the AA or RAC
    (b) a Customs-approved guarantor
    (c) the Export Credits Guarantee Department (ECGD)
    (d) the exporter's bankers

625. Community Transit guarantee vouchers are valid in which of the following non-EU countries?
    (a) Azerbaijan
    (b) Romania
    (c) Uzbekistan
    (d) Switzerland

626. HM Customs will accept guarantees given under Community Transit if they are provided by the:
    (a) Department of Trade and Industry
    (b) International Road Transport Union (IRU)
    (c) Road Haulage Association
    (d) Export Credits Guarantee Department (ECGD)

627. A Community Transit guarantee voucher:
    (a) exempts the exporter from Customs duty
    (b) saves exporters making individual deposits to cover any Customs claims
    (c) guarantees transit of goods across frontiers without Customs inspection
    (d) guarantees payment for export goods by the customer

628. Exporters consigning goods from the UK to the EU can avoid the need to lodge Customs deposits by using the system of:
    (a) Community Transit T2 declarations
    (b) TIR instead of Community Transit
    (c) Community Transit Article 41 procedure
    (d) Community Transit guarantee vouchers

629. The Community Transit procedure, which facilitates movement of goods within the EU, also covers the non-EU member state of:
    (a) Switzerland
    (b) Romania
    (c) Belarus
    (d) Norway

630. Under the Community Transit guarantee system, flat-rate guarantee vouchers can be obtained from the guarantor, each providing cover of up to:
(a) 2,500 units of account
(b) 3,000 units of account
(c) 5,000 units of account
(d) 7,000 units of account

631. To be sure they will get paid if a foreign customer defaults, an exporter will obtain:
(a) an ECGD certificate
(b) an ECMT permit
(c) a carnet de passage en douane
(d) CMR insurance cover

632. Certain operations under the full CT procedure do not need to be covered by guarantee. These include:
(a) where the consignment is shipped by both road and sea
(b) where the load is carried by a single vehicle for the whole journey
(c) when a CMR consignment note is in force
(d) transit between a UK office of departure and the first office of transit

633. An unplated semi-trailer dispatched unaccompanied to France for delivery would have to carry which of the following documents?
(a) a copy of Community Transit form T2
(b) an ATA carnet
(c) a carnet de passage en douane
(d) a TIR carnet

634. A full 8-part SAD set would be used for which of the following purposes?
(a) for export, Community Transit and import purposes
(b) for export declaration purposes only
(c) for import declaration purposes only
(d) for Community Transit purposes only

635. An exporter who does not wish to become directly involved with export procedures for their goods can put the whole operation into the hands of:
(a) the Freight Transport Association
(b) the Road Haulage Association
(c) the Chartered Institute of Transport
(d) a firm of freight forwarders

636. The RHA and FTA act as guarantors for liability for Customs duty on goods transported outside the EU by issuing:
    (a) TIR carnets
    (b) ATA carnets
    (c) carnets de passage en douane
    (d) ATP carnets

637. The SAD form in use throughout the Community comprises an 8-part set, certain copies of which remain in the country of dispatch while other copies travel forward with the goods. How many copies travel forward?
    (a) copies 1 to 3
    (b) copies 3 to 6
    (c) copies 2 to 6
    (d) copies 4 to 8

638. The document used to permit goods vehicles to pass through international frontiers, other than EU member states, without Customs examination is called a:
    (a) Community Transit consignment note
    (b) TIR carnet
    (c) CMR consignment note
    (d) SAD form

639. For non-EU road haulage movements the CT system is replaced by the:
    (a) AETR agreement
    (b) TIR convention
    (c) CMR convention
    (d) ATP convention

640. For which of the following countries would it not be necessary to produce a separate certificate of origin for the goods?
    (a) Turkey
    (b) Croatia
    (c) Greece
    (d) United Arab Emirates

641. A bill of lading is a document used:
    (a) to confirm that goods have been loaded on a ship
    (b) as a legal receipt for goods received for shipment
    (c) to confirm that a ship is loaded to capacity and is ready to sail
    (d) to show that goods are at the dockside ready for loading

642. An invoice approved by a representative of the country to which goods are being consigned is called a:
    (a) bill of lading
    (b) certified invoice
    (c) house bill
    (d) consular invoice

643. One of the main purposes for which consular invoices are required is to control:
    (a) illegal entry of import goods
    (b) illegal transfer of exchange currencies
    (c) payment of Customs duties
    (d) the influx of pornographic and illicit goods

TIR SYSTEM

644. TIR in the context of road transport is an international agreement to:
    (a) allow vehicles to cross national frontiers without Customs examination
    (b) control the movement of hazardous substances by road
    (c) control the movement of perishable goods by road
    (d) require international hauliers to be correctly covered by insurance

645. The TIR certificate of approval issued in respect of vehicles must be renewed:
    (a) annually
    (b) bi-annually
    (c) every 4 years
    (d) every 6 years

646. Vehicles operating internationally under the TIR convention must carry a:
    (a) valid TIR carnet only
    (b) valid TIR carnet and a certificate of approval for the vehicle
    (c) valid TIR carnet, a certificate of approval for the vehicle, and TIR plates front and rear
    (d) valid TIR carnet, and TIR plates front and rear

647. A TIR carnet is a document accepted as:
    (a) a bond against any Customs duties payable at frontier crossings
    (b) evidence that a bilateral road haulage permit exists for the journey

(c) evidence of insurance cover for international road haulage journeys

(d) evidence that the vehicle meets TIR approval standards

648. Unless an emergency situation arises, a driver should not break the TIR seals on their vehicle during the journey:
    (a) True
    (b) False

649. A TIR carnet contains a number of pages (volets) depending on the number of borders to be crossed on an international journey, but each full carnet covers:
    (a) a single outward load only
    (b) a single outward and return load
    (c) any number of outward journeys within the period of validity
    (d) any number of outward and return journeys within its validity

650. The main purpose of a TIR carnet is to ensure that the vehicle and load:
    (a) can be readily examined by Customs officials en route
    (b) can be Customs sealed during transit to prevent removals from or additions to the load
    (c) are correctly documented for export/import duty purposes
    (d) are correctly valued for international transport insurance purposes

651. To which of the following bodies is application made for inspection of vehicles for TIR approval purposes?
    (a) the International Road Freight Office
    (b) the VOSA, Goods Vehicle Centre, Swansea
    (c) the clerk to the Traffic Commissioner for the Traffic Area in which the vehicle is available for inspection
    (d) the manager of the nearest VOSA Goods Vehicle Test Station

652. Once a vehicle has received a TIR Certificate of Approval:
    (a) re-certification is necessary if it is transferred to a new owner
    (b) the Certificate can be transferred to a new owner without the vehicle having to be examined again for TIR approval purposes
    (c) the vehicle can be used by a new owner without re-certification during the two-year validity of the existing Certificate
    (d) it needs no further certification unless notifiable alterations are made to its structure

653. It is a legal requirement that vehicles used for international road haulage operations under the TIR Convention must:
    (a) display blue and white TIR plates at the front and rear
    (b) be certified as meeting the requirements of ADR
    (c) display an orange reflex reflecting marker plate at the rear
    (d) be certified as meeting the maintenance requirements of the Geneva Convention

654. A UK haulier on a journey to Greece via Germany, Austria and Croatia would need to use which of the following Customs systems?
    (a) the Greek national transit system
    (b) Transport International Routier (TIR)
    (c) Community Transit
    (d) ATA temporary importation

655. A 14-volet TIR carnet is valid for the international transportation of goods by road from the UK across a maximum of:
    (a) 6 frontiers
    (b) 7 frontiers
    (c) 10 frontiers
    (d) 14 frontiers

656. A vehicle with a TIR Certificate of Approval:
    (a) can be used on international journeys within the EU without a valid TIR carnet
    (b) must not travel to EU member states unless a valid TIR carnet is carried
    (c) may not be used on any international journey without a valid TIR carnet
    (d) must display blue on white TIR plates at all times

657. Which of the following organizations acts as a guarantor for TIR purposes and from which an operator would obtain a TIR carnet?
    (a) the London Chamber of Commerce
    (b) the DFt through local Traffic Area offices
    (c) the Freight Transport Association
    (d) the International Road Freight Office

658. TIR Certificates of Approval for goods vehicles are issued by the Department for Transport and the Regions on behalf of the:
    (a) European Customs Union (ECU)
    (b) RHA and FTA

(c) International Road Transport Union (IRU)
(d) European Council of Ministers of Transport (ECMT)

CARNETS

659. An ATA carnet is used for:
    (a) the temporary importation of goods
    (b) the temporary importation of vehicles/trailers
    (c) transit of goods on road/rail systems
    (d) establishing insurance liability for international loads

660. ATA carnets permit temporary importation of goods without payment of Customs duties or deposits and are applicable:
    (a) only to accompanied goods
    (b) only to unaccompanied goods
    (c) to both accompanied and unaccompanied goods
    (d) when permanent import of goods is required

661. The ATA Carnet scheme is accepted in which of the following countries?
    (a) CIS
    (b) Latvia
    (c) Turkey
    (d) Lithuania

662. ATA carnets may be obtained from which of the following organizations?
    (a) Chambers of Commerce in main cities
    (b) the RHA/FTA
    (c) the International Road Freight Office
    (d) the Department of Trade and Industry

CUSTOMS PROCEDURES

663. The Customs and Excise system whereby official control is exercised and records kept of goods to be exported abroad is known as:
    (a) prior export clearance
    (b) a simplified trade procedure
    (c) pre-entry
    (d) export trade recording

664. Which of the following organizations would issue a 'house' bill for an international consolidated load dispatched from the UK?
(a) the cross-channel ferry operator
(b) the customer's appointed freight agent
(c) HM Customs and Excise at the port of exit
(d) the International Road Freight Office

665. Which of the following categories of goods need not be pre-entered with HM Customs and Excise prior to export abroad?
(a) goods covered by the common agriculture policy (CAP)
(b) goods exported from a Customs and Excise bonded warehouse
(c) goods shipped under the simplified clearance procedure (SCP)
(d) goods for which an export licence is required

666. Which of the following goods must be pre-entered with HM Customs and Excise?
(a) exports from a Customs and Excise bonded warehouse
(b) export loads comprising hazardous substances
(c) consolidated loads consigned for export
(d) goods shipped under the simplified clearance procedure (SCP)

667. The copy of the SAD used for declaring imported goods is:
(a) copy 2
(b) copy 4
(c) copy 6
(d) copy 7

668. The pre-entry system under the SCP allows an exporter with a CRN to present the SAD document within a time limit of:
(a) 5 days
(b) 7 days
(c) 10 days
(d) 14 days

669. The Customs and Excise procedure for exporters who have a Customs-registered number (CRN) to provide statistical information is called:
(a) the simplified clearance procedure (SCP)
(b) the Community Transit (CT) procedure
(c) pre-entry
(d) CRN entry

670. Use of the single administrative document (SAD) in Customs procedures means that:
   (a) a single document can be used for worldwide export and import purposes
   (b) a single document can be used as an export/import declaration for trade with non-EU countries
   (c) a common single document is used for export and import declarations throughout all EU member states
   (d) the Community Transit (CT) system no longer applies to export consignments within the EU

671. Under the SCP pre-shipment advice requirement for export consignments HM Customs accept a CMR note, an FTA own-account document, or:
   (a) a Customs form C273
   (b) a Community Transit form T1
   (c) a carnet de passage en douane
   (d) Copy 2 of the SAD

672. The main reason for HM Customs requiring pre-entry of exports is to:
   (a) provide information for statistical purposes and to control the movement of prohibited goods
   (b) ensure that the haulier has the correct documentation for an international movement of an export consignment
   (c) ensure that the exporter has established a proper outlet for their goods abroad
   (d) ensure that correct levels of export duties are charged

673. Exporters who have registered and been allocated a Customs-registered number (CRN) may use the:
   (a) simplified clearance procedure (SCP)
   (b) TIR carnet procedure
   (c) Community Transit (CT) procedure
   (d) Customs commercial documentation procedure

674. For which of the following countries would the driver on an international journey be expected to have a form EUR 1 in respect of the goods carried?
   (a) Estonia
   (b) Norway
   (c) Italy
   (d) Latvia

675. An EU member state wishing to verify that goods being consigned for export are in free circulation within the Union would accept as proof:
    (a) an official certificate of origin
    (b) copy 4 of the SAD showing T2 status
    (c) the haulier's CMR note
    (d) copy 4 of the SAD showing T1 status

676. Which of the following would be used to establish the origin of goods made and exported from the UK to the EU but which is not accepted as a transit document:
    (a) Form T5 control copy
    (b) T2L procedure
    (c) T1 declaration on the SAD
    (d) T2 declaration on the SAD

677. Customs status T1 would apply to goods exported from the UK to other EU states which are:
    (a) not in free circulation within the Community
    (b) in free circulation within the Community
    (c) subject to special rates of import duty
    (d) allowed entry free of duty in any country

CHAPTER 10

Typical questions:
Technical standards and
aspects of operation

(covering syllabus sections G1 to G10)

VEHICLE WEIGHTS AND DIMENSIONS

678. The weight of a vehicle, inclusive of body and parts normally used in its operation but exclusive of the weight of water, fuel, loose tools and equipment, and batteries used for propulsion, is defined as the:
    (a) plated weight
    (b) unladen weight
    (c) tare weight
    (d) kerb weight

679. The total weight legally imposed on a road by a vehicle including driver, load, fuel, water and loose tools is the:
    (a) kerb weight
    (b) payload
    (c) unladen weight
    (d) gross vehicle weight

680. The weight of a goods vehicle in road-going condition, inclusive of oil, water and fuel but without its load and without the driver, is defined as the:
(a) tare weight
(b) kerb weight
(c) unladen weight
(d) gross vehicle weight

681. When entering premises to collect bulk loads, vehicles usually cross a weighbridge to establish the weight of the empty vehicle complete with driver. This weight is the:
(a) tare weight
(b) kerb weight
(c) maximum laden weight
(d) gross train weight

682. When calculating the maximum payload for a goods vehicle it is necessary to deduct the:
(a) kerb weight from the maximum laden weight
(b) unladen weight from the gross train weight
(c) tare weight from the permissible maximum weight
(d) maximum laden weight from the gross vehicle weight

683. When determining the tare weight of a goods vehicle by weighing prior to loading, the weight should include:
(a) the driver, any passengers and a full tank of fuel
(b) any passengers to be carried and a full tank of fuel
(c) the driver only; passengers and fuel to be added later
(d) no driver or passengers and a low tank of fuel

684. The payload capacity of a vehicle is calculated by deducting its kerb weight from the:
(a) unladen weight
(b) gross vehicle weight
(c) total of axle weight
(d) gross plated weight

685. In calculating the unladen weight of a vehicle which uses alternative bodies which of the following applies?
(a) the weight of the heaviest alternative body must be included
(b) the weight of the lightest of alternative body must be included
(c) the weight of the body most frequently used is included
(d) the weight of such bodies is not included

686. The maximum permitted weight at which a rigid goods vehicle may be used on roads in the UK is the:
    (a) gross combination weight
    (b) gross plated weight
    (c) gross train weight
    (d) kerb weight

687. A 'motor car' is defined in law as a mechanically propelled vehicle constructed to carry goods or passengers and with an unladen weight not exceeding:
    (a) 1,525 kg
    (b) 2,030 kg
    (c) 2,540 kg
    (d) 3,050 kg

688. The term 'relevant axle spacing' used in connection with weight calculations for articulated vehicles means the distance between the:
    (a) rear axle of the tractive unit and the rear axle of the semi-trailer
    (b) rear axle of the tractive unit and the front axle of the semi-trailer
    (c) front axle of the tractive unit and the front axle of the semi-trailer
    (d) front axle of the tractive unit and the rear axle of the semi-trailer

689. A vehicle with a wheelbase of 6 metres is carrying a uniform load of 9,000 kg. If the centreline of the load is 3.0 metres from the front axle the weight on the rear axle will be:
    (a) 4,500 kg
    (b) 5,000 kg
    (c) 5,600 kg
    (d) 5,800 kg

690. A vehicle carrying a uniform load of 6 tonnes has a wheelbase of 6 metres. If the distance from the centre of the load to the rear axle is 2 metres the weight on the front axle will be:
    (a) 2 tonnes
    (b) 3 tonnes
    (c) 5 tonnes
    (d) 7 tonnes

691. The maximum weight for an axle fitted with two wheels in line transversely, each equipped with twin tyres having centres not less than 300 mm apart, on a vehicle is:
    (a) 9,200 kg
    (b) 10,170 kg
    (c) 11,000 kg
    (d) 11,500 kg

692. The maximum weight that may be imposed on a single-wheel axle where there is no other wheel in line transversely is:
(a) 5,090 kg
(b) 4,600 kg
(c) 9,200 kg
(d) 1,020 kg

693. Where a vehicle is fitted with a bogie comprising two closely spaced axles at least 1.85 metres apart and the plated weight of neither axle exceeds half the specified weight, the maximum weight for the bogie is:
(a) 18,800 kg
(b) 19,320 kg
(c) 20,000 kg
(d) 20,340 kg

694. For a vehicle/trailer fitted with three adjacent axles having at least 4.6 metres between the foremost and rearmost axles, the maximum total weight permitted on the axles is:
(a) 18,290 kg
(b) 20,330 kg
(c) 22,360 kg
(d) 24,000 kg

695. If a tri-axle bogie on a semi-trailer is equipped with air suspension, the maximum weight permitted on each individual axle is:
(a) 6.0 tonnes
(b) 7.5 tonnes
(c) 8.0 tonnes
(d) 9.0 tonnes

696. When calculating the overall length of a vehicle, which of the following items is excluded from the calculation?
(a) vehicle headlamps and fog lamps
(b) a tailboard let down to facilitate loading
(c) front-mounted towing eyes
(d) rear under-run bumper

697. The permitted maximum overall length for an articulated vehicle (not designed to carry indivisible loads of exceptional length) in the UK is:
(a) 11.5 metres
(b) 12 metres
(c) 15.5 metres
(d) 16.5 metres

698. The permitted maximum overall length for a road train in the UK comprising a rigid vehicle and drawbar trailer is:
(a) 15 metres
(b) 16.5 metres
(c) 18.75 metres
(d) 18.5 metres

699. The height of a vehicle and its load travelling through the Netherlands and Germany should not exceed:
(a) 3.5 metres
(b) 4.0 metres
(c) 4.2 metres
(d) 4.5 metres

700. The current maximum length permitted for a road train in Europe is:
(a) 15.5 metres
(b) 16.5 metres
(c) 18.0 metres
(d) 18.75 metres

701. The maximum permitted length for a UK articulated vehicle used on international journeys is:
(a) 16.5 metres
(b) 12.2 metres
(c) not restricted
(d) any length provided that the load-carrying space does not exceed 12.2 metres

702. The maximum overall length for a vehicle and load permitted by the Special Types General Order is:
(a) 15.5 metres
(b) 16.5 metres
(c) 18.3 metres
(d) 27.4 metres

703. The maximum permitted length for a 2-axle rigid goods vehicle is:
(a) 11 metres
(b) 12 metres
(c) 15.5 metres
(d) 18 metres

704. The maximum permitted length for a composite trailer used in transport operations is:
    (a) 12.2 metres
    (b) 14.04 metres
    (c) 16.5 metres
    (d) not limited providing the combination does not exceed 15.5 metres

705. The maximum permitted length for a 3-axle rigid goods vehicle is:
    (a) 11 metres
    (b) 12 metres
    (c) 13.6 metres
    (d) 15 metres

706. Which of the following must be included when determining the overall width of a heavy goods vehicle?
    (a) rear-view driving mirrors
    (b) bodywork protection rubbing strakes
    (c) a sideboard let down to facilitate loading
    (d) a receptacle to contain a Customs seal

707. The maximum permitted width for a normal goods vehicle exceeding 3.5 tonnes is:
    (a) 2.0 metres
    (b) 2.3 metres
    (c) 2.55 metres
    (d) 2.75 metres

708. The maximum overall width for a vehicle defined as a 'heavy motor car' must not exceed:
    (a) 2.1 metres
    (b) 2.3 metres
    (c) 2.55 metres
    (d) 2.75 metres

709. The maximum permitted width of a trailer being drawn by a motor vehicle not exceeding 2 tonnes unladen weight is:
    (a) 2.3 metres
    (b) 2.5 metres
    (c) 2.6 metres
    (d) 2.75 metres

710. The maximum width for an articulated combination comprising a tractive unit and refrigerated semi-trailer is:
(a) 12.5 metres
(b) 12.75 metres
(c) 2.55 metres
(d) 2.6 metres

711. The maximum overhang permitted for rigid goods vehicles is:
(a) 50 per cent of the wheelbase
(b) 55 per cent of the wheelbase
(c) 60 per cent of the wheelbase
(d) 65 per cent of the wheelbase

712. The overhang of a 3-axled vehicle with a tandem rear bogie is measured from:
(a) the centreline between the rear axles
(b) a point 100 mm behind the centreline between the rear axles
(c) a point 110 mm behind the centreline between the rear axles
(d) a point 110 mm ahead of the centreline between the rear axles

713. For the purposes of ensuring proper axle-weight distribution, the removal of part of the load from the rear overhang of a laden goods vehicle will:
(a) increase the load on both the front and rear axles
(b) reduce the load on both the front and rear axles
(c) decrease loading on the front axle and increase it on the rear axle
(d) increase loading on the front axle and decrease it on the rear axle

714. The permitted maximum weight for a rigid goods vehicle with four or more axles is:
(a) 26,420 kg
(b) 28,450 kg
(c) 32,000 kg
(d) 32,520 kg

715. The total weight transmitted to the road surface by any two wheels in line transversely on an axle fitted with single tyres must not exceed:
(a) 9,000 kg
(b) 9,100 kg
(c) 9,200 kg
(d) 9,500 kg

716. A 5-axled articulated vehicle comprising a 2-axle tractive unit and tri-axle semi-trailer with a relevant axle spacing of at least 6.9 metres has a permissible maximum weight under the AW regulations of:
    (a) 32,520 kg
    (b) 35,000 kg
    (c) 36,000 kg
    (d) 40,000 kg

717. The maximum permitted AW weight for a 2-axled rigid goods vehicle is:
    (a) 13,230 kg
    (b) 14,230 kg
    (c) 18,000 kg
    (d) 18,230 kg

718. An articulated vehicle with a single-axle semi-trailer and with a relevant axle spacing of 2.9 metres has a maximum permitted C&U weight of:
    (a) 20,330 kg
    (b) 23,370 kg
    (c) 26,000 kg
    (d) 32,520 kg

719. In calculating the maximum permitted weight for an 8-wheel rigid goods vehicle it is necessary to know the distance between the:
    (a) two front steering axles
    (b) two axles of the rear bogie
    (c) rearmost front axle and the foremost rear axle
    (d) foremost axle and the rearmost axle

720. As a general rule the wider the axle spacings on a goods vehicle, the greater the permissible maximum weight:
    (a) True
    (b) False

721. The gross train weight shown on the 'Ministry' plate attached to an articulated tractive unit is the total weight permitted in the UK for:
    (a) the tractive unit only
    (b) the semi-trailer and load
    (c) both the tractive unit and loaded semi-trailer
    (d) the load permitted to be carried on the vehicle

722. If P = payload, W = wheelbase and D = distance from the centre-line of the payload to the rear axle, then the load on the front axle is calculated by using the formula:

(a) $\dfrac{P + D}{W}$

(b) $\dfrac{P \times D}{W}$

(c) $\dfrac{W \times D}{P}$

(d) $\dfrac{W \times P}{D}$

723. The gross weight of a rigid goods vehicle is the:
    (a) maximum weight at which the vehicle is legally permitted to operate
    (b) total weight transmitted to the road by all the wheels of the laden vehicle
    (c) total weight of an unladen vehicle
    (d) total weight of a rigid vehicle and loaded drawbar trailer

724. Which of the following is classed in law as a 'small goods vehicle'?
    (a) a vehicle constructed to carry goods with a permissible maximum weight of 7 tonnes and drawing a trailer of 2 tonnes gross weight
    (b) a vehicle constructed to carry goods with a permissible maximum weight of 3 tonnes and drawing a trailer of 1 tonne gross weight
    (c) a vehicle constructed to carry goods with a permissible maximum weight of 2.5 tonnes and drawing a trailer of 1 tonne gross weight
    (d) a vehicle constructed to carry goods with a permissible maximum weight of 3,550 kg

725. A goods vehicle is legally defined as a 'motor car' if its unladen weight does not exceed:
    (a) 2,500 kg
    (b) 2,750 kg
    (c) 3,050 kg
    (d) 3,500 kg

726. A 'composite trailer' as defined in law is a combination of:
    (a) a converter dolly and an articulated semi-trailer
    (b) a converter dolly and a drawbar trailer
    (c) two semi-trailers joined together behind a rigid motor vehicle
    (d) two drawbar trailers joined together behind a motor vehicle

727. An articulated vehicle is defined in law as a heavy motor car with a trailer so attached that when the trailer is uniformly loaded a proportion of the weight of the load is transferred to the drawing vehicle amounting to:
(a) 10 per cent
(b) 15 per cent
(c) 20 per cent
(d) 25 per cent

728. The abbreviation GTW means:
(a) gross tare weight
(b) gross train weight
(c) gross trailer weight
(d) gross towing weight

729. The abbreviation GCW means:
(a) gross carrying weight
(b) gross combination weight
(c) gross chartered weight
(d) greater capacity weight

730. The term GTW applies to the gross weight of:
(a) a towing vehicle
(b) an articulated tractive unit
(c) a semi-trailer
(d) a vehicle and trailer combination

731. A 'medium-sized goods vehicle' is defined in law as a vehicle constructed or adapted for the carriage of goods and which has a gross weight of between:
(a) 2.5 tonnes and 5 tonnes
(b) 3.0 tonnes and 5 tonnes
(c) 3.5 tonnes and 7 tonnes
(d) 3.5 tonnes and 7.5 tonnes

732. A 'heavy motor car' is defined in law as a mechanically propelled vehicle not being a motor car which is constructed to carry a load or passengers and with an unladen weight exceeding:
(a) 1,525 kg
(b) 2,540 kg
(c) 3,500 kg
(d) 7,500 kg

VEHICLE SPECIFICATIONS

733. Selecting a heavy goods vehicle to achieve environmental objectives means choosing one with:
    (a) steel spring suspension
    (b) high axle loadings
    (c) a Reduced Pollution Certificate
    (d) a standard exhaust system

VEHICLE CONDITION AND FITNESS

734. Application for heavy goods vehicle annual tests are made to:
    (a) the local VOSA Goods Vehicle Testing Station
    (b) the Goods Vehicle Centre, Swansea
    (c) the TC for the Traffic Area in which the vehicle is kept
    (d) the Local Vehicle Registration Office

735. Heavy goods vehicle plating and annual testing applies to rigid goods vehicles over:
    (a) 1,020 kg unladen weight
    (b) 1,525 kg unladen weight
    (c) 1,750 kg unladen weight
    (d) 3,500 kg gross weight

736. Under the regulations dealing with goods vehicle plating and annual testing, a part IV examination is:
    (a) a test following a notifiable alteration to the vehicle
    (b) re-examination of a vehicle following failure of a first test
    (c) re-examination of a vehicle following failure of a periodical test
    (d) re-examination of a vehicle following appeal against a test failure

737. To which of the following types of vehicle do the goods vehicle plating and annual testing regulations apply?
    (a) articulated semi-trailers
    (b) breakdown vehicles
    (c) electrically propelled motor vehicles
    (d) engineering plant

738. Which of the following are exempt from goods vehicle plating and annual testing?
    (a) vehicles first registered before 1 January 1961 and used unladen
    (b) vehicles operated for the purposes of telecommunications
    (c) refuse collection vehicles operated by a local authority
    (d) electrically propelled motor vehicles

739. The maximum gross weight at which a vehicle may be plated is reduced if it is fitted with tyres of a lower weight rating:
(a) True
(b) False

740. Under the goods vehicle plating and annual testing regulations, which of the following alterations must be notified to the Goods Vehicle Centre before the vehicle is used on the road?
(a) a change of registered keeper
(b) any change in the vehicle braking system
(c) a change of use
(d) a change of colour

741. The maximum gross weight at which a goods vehicle is plated is determined by:
(a) the vehicle manufacturer
(b) the Traffic Commissioner
(c) the Goods Vehicle Centre in conjunction with the manufacturer
(d) the Driver and Vehicle Licensing Agency, Swansea

742. A manufacturer's plate must be fitted to all goods vehicles (with certain exceptions) first used on or after 1 January 1968:
(a) True
(b) False

743. Where a vehicle displays both a manufacturer's plate and a 'Ministry' plate, the former takes precedence over the latter:
(a) True
(b) False

744. Which of the following items of information is not found on a 'Ministry' goods vehicle plate?
(a) the year of manufacture of the vehicle
(b) the maximum permissible weights not to be exceeded in GB
(c) the manufacturer's name and address
(d) the weights for all axles of the vehicle

745. A goods vehicle testing station may refuse to test a vehicle or trailer for which of the following reasons?
(a) the driver did not produce a valid certificate of insurance
(b) the vehicle was in a dirty condition
(c) the vehicle was not accompanied by a competent motor fitter
(d) it had been painted a different colour since the previous test

746. VOSA may issue certificates of temporary exemption from goods vehicle annual testing requirements for a period not exceeding:
(a) 1 month
(b) 3 months
(c) 6 months
(d) 12 months

747. If a goods vehicle fails the annual test it may be re-submitted to the same test station for re-examination of the defective components only within:
(a) 1 week
(b) 8 days
(c) 14 days
(d) 3 weeks

748. Appeals against the results of a goods vehicle annual test should be made in the first instance to:
(a) the local VOSA technical officer
(b) the Goods Vehicle Test Station manager
(c) the Secretary of State for Transport
(d) the Goods Vehicle Centre, Swansea

749. Which of the following items need not be shown on a manufacturer's plate?
(a) the number of axles
(b) the vehicle type
(c) tyre ply ratings and maximum pressures
(d) maximum gross weight

750. Vehicles subject to goods vehicle annual testing must generally be submitted for their first annual test:
(a) by the third anniversary of the month of their original registration
(b) before the beginning of the first anniversary month of their original registration
(c) before the end of the first anniversary month of their original registration
(d) before the end of the first anniversary month of their date of manufacture

751. Following a first annual test of a goods vehicle, subsequent annual tests are due:
    (a) each year by the end of the anniversary month of the date of their first registration
    (b) by the expiry date of the existing test certificate
    (c) in the anniversary month of their date of original manufacture
    (d) on a date allocated by the Goods Vehicle Centre, Swansea

752. Which of the following items need not be shown on the manufacturer's plate fitted to a goods-carrying trailer?
    (a) maximum gross weight
    (b) year of original manufacture
    (c) trailer chassis number
    (d) place of manufacture

753. In exceptional circumstances, where it is not possible to have a vehicle tested by the due date, a temporary exemption certificate may be issued valid for:
    (a) 3 months
    (b) 6 months
    (c) 12 months
    (d) 15 months

754. Goods vehicles subject to plating and annual testing become due for their first test:
    (a) in the 6th month after original registration
    (b) in the 11th month after original registration
    (c) by the end of the 1st anniversary month of the date of first registration
    (d) in the month following the anniversary of their first registration

755. One of the grounds on which a goods vehicle test station can refuse to test a vehicle is:
    (a) if it is in a dirty condition
    (b) if the driver is not accompanied by a skilled fitter
    (c) if it is laden
    (d) if an articulated vehicle arrives with a semi-trailer attached

756. Which of the following is not a notifiable alteration under goods vehicle plating and annual testing?
    (a) fitting an extra axle to increase the vehicle carrying capacity
    (b) an alteration which increases the rear overhang by more than one foot
    (c) fitting a body of a different construction
    (d) fitting tyres of a different make

757. Where a goods vehicle operator carries out a notifiable alteration on their vehicle, they must:
(a) advise the Goods Vehicle Centre, Swansea
(b) send the vehicle registration document to Swansea for amendment
(c) apply for a new plate and plating certificate
(d) obtain a new Type Approval certificate

758. In accordance with the Freight Containers (Safety Convention) Regulations 1984, safety approval plates for freight containers are issued by:
(a) the Road Haulage Association
(b) VOSA Goods Vehicle Test Stations
(c) a body appointed by the Health and Safety Executive
(d) Lloyds Register of Shipping

759. A Certificate of Conformity relating to a vehicle indicates that it conforms to:
(a) Type Approval standards
(b) a specified British Standard
(c) a BS Quality Standard
(d) goods vehicle plating requirements

760. Since the introduction of Type Approval, goods vehicles subject to plating and annual testing are issued with a 'Ministry' plate:
(a) at the point of manufacture
(b) when first presented for annual test
(c) when first specified on a goods vehicle 'O' licence
(d) when first registered

CONSTRUCTION AND USE OF VEHICLES

761. Which of the following is covered by the goods vehicle Type Approval regulations?
(a) exhaust emissions
(b) the aim of vehicle headlights
(c) the strength of rear bumpers
(d) the ply rating for tyres

762. National Type Approval for goods vehicles is also applicable to:
(a) locomotives
(b) motor tractors
(c) breakdown vehicles
(d) 4-wheel-drive dual-purpose vehicles

763. If the fuel tank supplying petrol for an engine used to drive ancillary equipment on a vehicle is made of plastic:
    (a) there is no contravention of the law
    (b) the law is contravened because the fuel should be supplied from the main tank
    (c) the law is contravened because the fuel tank should be made of metal to conform to C&U regulations requirements
    (d) the law is contravened because ancillary equipment should only be driven by diesel fuel

764. Excess fuel devices fitted to diesel-engined vehicles must not be used when the vehicle is in motion:
    (a) True
    (b) False

765. Which of the following items is not covered by the road vehicles C&U regulations?
    (a) windscreen washers and wipers
    (b) rear-view mirrors
    (c) vehicle registration plates
    (d) windscreen glass

766. It is an offence to sound the horn of a motor vehicle on a restricted road between:
    (a) 22.30 hours and 07.30 hours
    (b) 23.30 hours and 07.30 hours
    (c) 23.00 hours and 07.00 hours
    (d) 23.30 hours and 07.00 hours

767. The law requiring a road vehicle to have an audible warning device does not apply to:
    (a) a moped
    (b) vehicles used under a trade licence
    (c) military vehicles
    (d) a vehicle not capable of exceeding 20 mph on the level

768. Gongs, bells and two-tone horns are not permitted on:
    (a) vehicles used by the police
    (b) military vehicles used for bomb-disposal purposes
    (c) breakdown vehicles used for emergency recovery work
    (d) vehicles used by the Blood Transfusion Service

769. Goods vehicles must be fitted with:
   (a) three mirrors, two fitted externally and one internally
   (b) two mirrors fitted externally on the offside and on the nearside
   (c) two mirrors, one fitted internally and one externally on the nearside
   (d) two mirrors, one externally on the offside and the other fitted either internally or externally on the nearside

770. Where two rear-view mirrors are required on goods vehicles to comply with the law they must show traffic:
   (a) to the rear only
   (b) to the rear and nearside rearwards
   (c) to the rear and offside rearwards
   (d) to the rear and both sides rearwards

771. Seat belts must be fitted to which of the following vehicles?
   (a) taxis and private-hire vehicles
   (b) vehicles being driven on a road test under a trade licence
   (c) a light van first registered since 1 April 1967
   (d) a goods vehicle with a maximum gross weight of 3,550 kg

772. When a broken-down vehicle is being towed by means of a rope or chain, the maximum distance permitted between the two vehicles is:
   (a) 1.5 metres
   (b) 4.0 metres
   (c) 4.5 metres
   (d) 5 metres

773. Spray suppression devices must be fitted to all trailers built since 1 May 1985 and which have a maximum gross weight exceeding:
   (a) 3.5 tonnes
   (b) 7.5 tonnes
   (c) 10 tonnes
   (d) 16 tonnes

774. Spray suppression devices must be fitted to all new goods vehicles first used since 1 April 1986 and exceeding:
   (a) 7.5 tonnes gross weight
   (b) 10 tonnes gross weight
   (c) 12 tonnes gross weight
   (d) 16 tonnes gross weight

775. Sideguards are legally required on new goods vehicles exceeding 3,500 kg maximum gross weight if the distance between any two consecutive axles exceeds:
(a) 2.0 metres
(b) 2.5 metres
(c) 3.0 metres
(d) 3.5 metres

776. Rear under-run protection is required on most new rigid goods vehicles where the maximum gross weight exceeds:
(a) 1,020 kg
(b) 1,525 kg
(c) 2,040 kg
(d) 3,500 kg

777. Rear under-run protection is not required on goods vehicles incapable of exceeding a maximum speed on a level road of:
(a) 10mph
(b) 15mph
(c) 20mph
(d) 25mph

778. Rear under-run protection is required on goods-carrying trailers manufactured on or after 1 May 1983 and with an unladen weight exceeding:
(a) 1,020 kg
(b) 2,040 kg
(c) 3,500 kg
(d) 750 kg

779. The maximum noise level permitted for a light goods vehicle 'in use' is:
(a) 81 decibels
(b) 84 decibels
(c) 87 decibels
(d) 92 decibels

780. Regulations require vehicles to be equipped with safety glass in the:
(a) windscreen only
(b) windscreen and windows to the front
(c) windscreen, windows to the front and on the offside of the driver's seat
(d) windscreen, windows to the front and on either side of the driver's seat

781. Vehicle C&U regulations require vehicles having a windscreen to be fitted with:
   (a) one efficient automatic windscreen wiper
   (b) one or more efficient automatic windscreen wipers
   (c) at least two efficient automatic windscreen wipers
   (d) an adequate method of clearing the windscreen

782. A driver who stopped at a motorway service station found when they returned to their vehicle that vandals had damaged the windscreen wipers. The law:
   (a) requires the driver to leave the motorway at the next available exit
   (b) requires the driver to notify the police before proceeding to the nearest garage for repairs
   (c) allows the driver complete their journey before having the wipers repaired
   (d) prohibits the driver from taking the vehicle on the public highway until the wipers are repaired and function efficiently

783. It is not an offence to drive a motor vehicle without efficient windscreen wipers:
   (a) when it is not raining
   (b) if the vehicle is not capable of travelling at more than 30 mph
   (c) if the driver can obtain an adequate view to the front without looking through the windscreen
   (d) if the vehicle was first registered before 1 January 1940

784. Legal requirements regarding the fitment of pneumatic tyres on motor vehicles do not apply to:
   (a) vehicles incapable of travelling at more than 20 mph
   (b) vehicles operated under a trade licence
   (c) vehicles being towed to a scrapyard to be broken up
   (d) vehicles used mainly for work on rough ground

785. Regulations currently specify a minimum depth for the tread of tyres on over-3.5-tonne motor vehicles of:
   (a) 1 mm
   (b) 1.5 mm
   (c) 1.6 mm
   (d) 2.1 mm

786. The minimum tread depth specified in law for tyres fitted to motor vehicles and trailers must extend to:
    (a) the whole breadth and around three-quarters of the circumference
    (b) three-quarters of the breadth and around the entire circumference
    (c) the whole breadth and around the entire circumference
    (d) half the breadth and around the entire circumference

787. A 'wide tyre' as defined in regulations is one having a minimum width in contact with the road surface of:
    (a) 200 mm
    (b) 250 mm
    (c) 300 mm
    (d) 350 mm

788. Regulations state that a pneumatic tyre fitted to a motor vehicle must not have a cut deep enough to reach the ply or cord in excess of:
    (a) 10 per cent of the section width
    (b) 25 mm or 10 per cent of the section width
    (c) 25 mm or 15 per cent of the section width
    (d) 25 mm or 20 per cent of the section width

789. Re-cut tyres may be used on vehicles legally defined as 'motor cars' providing the wheel-rim diameter exceeds:
    (a) 300 mm
    (b) 305 mm
    (c) 400 mm
    (d) 405 mm

790. Motor vehicles first used since 1 January 1968 must have a service brake with a minimum efficiency of:
    (a) 45 per cent
    (b) 50 per cent
    (c) 55 per cent
    (d) 60 per cent

791. In the event of failure of one part of a split braking system on a vehicle, the remaining part of the system must have an efficiency of not less than:
    (a) 25 per cent
    (b) 30 per cent
    (c) 40 per cent
    (d) 45 per cent

792. The minimum specified braking efficiencies for pre-1968 motor vehicles drawing a trailer are:
    (a) service brake 35 per cent and secondary brake 15 per cent
    (b) service brake 45 per cent and secondary brake 20 per cent
    (c) service brake 45 per cent and secondary brake 25 per cent
    (d) service brake 50 per cent and secondary brake 25 per cent

793. A new vehicle with a permissible maximum weight of 16 tonnes has a service braking system with an efficiency of 45 per cent and a secondary system with an efficiency of 25 per cent. Legal requirements are met by:
    (a) both braking systems
    (b) the service braking system only
    (c) the secondary braking system only
    (d) neither braking system

794. The law requires new goods vehicles to have a parking brake capable of holding the vehicle (without the assistance of stored energy) on a gradient of at least:
    (a) 12 per cent
    (b) 16 per cent
    (c) 25 per cent
    (d) 50 per cent

795. The parking brake of new motor cars and heavy motor cars drawing trailers must be capable of holding the vehicle and any trailer attached on a maximum gradient of:
    (a) 10 per cent
    (b) 12 per cent
    (c) 16 per cent
    (d) 25 per cent

796. Which vehicle and trailer combination may legally be used on a public road?
    (a) a rigid goods vehicle drawing 2 unladen trailers
    (b) a rigid goods vehicle drawing 1 laden and 1 unladen trailer
    (c) a rigid goods vehicle drawing 1 laden trailer
    (d) a motor tractor drawing 2 laden trailers

797. When a broken-down vehicle has to be towed, the law requires the:
    (a) towing vehicle to display an amber flashing beacon
    (b) towed vehicle to display the words 'on tow' at the rear
    (c) towing vehicle to travel with its headlamps illuminated
    (d) registration mark of the towing vehicle to be displayed on the rear of the towed vehicle

798. A vehicle defined in law as a locomotive may draw 2 laden trailers:
    (a) True
    (b) False

799. A towing vehicle with a permissible maximum weight not exceeding 3,500 kg is permitted to tow a trailer with a maximum length of:
    (a) 5 metres
    (b) 7 metres
    (c) 11 metres
    (d) 12 metres

VEHICLE LIGHTING

800. Lighting regulations require which of the following lamps to be fitted to all goods vehicles?
    (a) 2 front-mounted spot or fog lamps
    (b) 2 rear fog lamps
    (c) 1 rear number plate lamp
    (d) 1 or 2 reversing lamps

801. When driving a vehicle during daylight hours which has a defective front position lamp the legal situation is that:
    (a) the driver will not be convicted of an offence if he can prove that the light became defective during the journey in progress
    (b) no offence is committed if the other vehicle lights remain operational
    (c) an offence is committed because all vehicle lights must be in good working order at all times
    (d) an offence will only be committed if the vehicle is driven between sunset and sunrise or in poor daytime visibility

802. Under current vehicle lighting regulations, vehicle lights must be used from:
    (a) sunset to sunrise
    (b) half an hour after sunset to half an hour after sunrise
    (c) half an hour before sunset to half an hour before sunrise
    (d) an hour after sunset to an hour before sunrise

803. With certain exceptions, goods vehicles first used on or after 1 April 1980 must be fitted with at least:
    (a) one rear fog lamp
    (b) two rear fog lamps
    (c) one front-mounted spot lamp
    (d) two front-mounted fog lamps

804. Two rear red stop lamps are required on all motor vehicles first used since:
(a) 1 January 1970
(b) 1 December 1970
(c) 1 January 1971
(d) 1 December 1971

805. Vehicle lighting regulations require obligatory dipped-beam headlamps to be fitted at a maximum distance from the side of the vehicle of:
(a) 400 mm
(b) 500 mm
(c) 600 mm
(d) 700 mm

806. Regulations require that obligatory headlamps on new vehicles must be fitted not less and not more than specified distances from the ground of:
(a) 300 mm and 600 mm
(b) 400 mm and 800 mm
(c) 500 mm and 1000 mm
(d) 500 mm and 1200 mm

807. Dipped-beam headlamps must be fitted to all vehicles capable of travelling at a speed in excess of:
(a) 5 mph
(b) 10 mph
(c) 15 mph
(d) 20 mph

808. Obligatory headlamps must be used during the hours of darkness in any unlit area where the street lamps are positioned more than:
(a) 150 yards apart
(b) 200 yards apart
(c) 225 yards apart
(d) 250 yards apart

809. A matching pair of correctly mounted front fog lamps may be used in place of dipped headlamps:
(a) not at all
(b) in severely reduced visibility at any time
(c) in severely reduced visibility during the hours of darkness
(d) only in conditions of fog or falling snow

810. Where front position lamps are required by law to be fitted to trailers drawn by motor vehicles they must be positioned:
    (a) a maximum distance of 150 mm from the side
    (b) a minimum distance of 300 mm from the side
    (c) a minimum distance of 450 mm from the side
    (d) a maximum distance of 450 mm from the side

811. Side marker lamps must be carried on each side of the vehicle or load where the total length of the vehicle or combination of vehicles exceeds:
    (a) 13 metres
    (b) 15 metres
    (c) 18.3 metres
    (d) 20.3 metres

812. It is a requirement that British vehicles travelling through France must comply with French lighting regulations for headlights to be yellow:
    (a) True
    (b) False

813. The 1989 vehicle lighting regulations require side marker lamps to be fitted to trailers with an overall length exceeding:
    (a) 8.15 metres
    (b) 9.15 metres
    (c) 9.45 metres
    (d) 10.0 metres

814. Side marker lamps are required when two vehicles in combination (other than an articulated vehicle) are carrying a supported load where the overall length inclusive of the load:
    (a) is between 12.2 metres and 18.3 metres
    (b) exceeds 18.3 metres
    (c) does not exceed 12.2 metres
    (d) exceeds 25.9 metres

815. The maximum wattage permitted by regulations for a reversing lamp not bearing an approval mark is:
    (a) 7 watts
    (b) 21 watts
    (c) 24 watts
    (d) 30 watts

816. Vehicle lighting regulations limit the wattage of stop lamps (other than those bearing an approval mark) fitted to post-1971 registered vehicles to:
(a) 5 to 15 watts
(b) 10 to 25 watts
(c) 15 to 36 watts
(d) a minimum of 36 watts

817. The law requires fitment of amber side-facing retro-reflectors to normal rigid goods vehicles first registered since 1 April 1986 and exceeding a length of:
(a) 6 metres
(b) 8 metres
(c) 9 metres
(d) 11 metres

818. Two amber side-facing retro-reflectors must be fitted on each side of trailers longer than:
(a) 4.5 metres
(b) 5 metres
(c) 6 metres
(d) 9 metres

819. Regulations limit the minimum and maximum height above the ground for the fitment of amber side-facing retro-reflectors on vehicles to between:
(a) 400 mm and 1,000 mm
(b) 500 mm and 1,200 mm
(c) 600 mm and 1,500 mm
(d) 350 mm and 1,500 mm

820. Which of the following vehicles must legally display amber light from a rotating beacon?
(a) private ambulances
(b) breakdown vehicles attending a roadside breakdown
(c) breakdown vehicles while towing a disabled vehicle
(d) vehicles not capable of exceeding 25 mph

821. The rate at which direction indicator lamps must flash is between:
(a) 50 and 100 times per minute
(b) 60 and 100 times per minute
(c) 60 and 120 times per minute
(d) 60 and 130 times per minute

822. To meet the legal requirements for direction indicators, vehicles first used since 1 April 1986 must be fitted with:
(a) 1 side indicator on each side
(b) 1 shoulder indicator and 1 rear indicator on each side
(c) 1 front and 1 rear indicator on each side
(d) 1 front, 1 rear and 1 side repeater indicator on each side

823. Rear reflective markings of red fluorescent and yellow reflective material must be fitted to rigid goods vehicles first registered after 1 August 1982 which exceed:
(a) 3,500 kg maximum gross weight
(b) 6,000 kg maximum gross weight
(c) 7,500 kg maximum gross weight
(d) 8,000 kg maximum gross weight

824. Which of the following classes of vehicle is exempt from the need to be fitted with rear reflective markers?
(a) goods vehicles over 7.5 tonnes gross
(b) trailers over 3.5 tonnes gross
(c) vehicles operating on trade plates
(d) articulated tractive units

825. Diagonal rear reflective markers may be fitted to which of the following vehicles or trailers?
(a) rigid vehicles more than 13 metres long
(b) trailers in combination more than 13 metres long
(c) rigid vehicles not more than 13 metres long
(d) trailers in combination more than 16.5 metres long

826. A red and yellow rear reflective marker displaying the words 'LONG VEHICLE' may be displayed at the rear of a trailer in combination exceeding:
(a) 11 metres
(b) 12 metres
(c) 13 metres
(d) 15 metres

827. When positioning lights on rearward projecting loads the light must be fitted a specified distance measured from the:
(a) rearmost point of the vehicle
(b) existing vehicle rear lamps
(c) existing vehicle rear reflectors
(d) rearmost projection of the load

828. A vehicle which carries a load projecting 450 mm beyond each side must display between sunset and sunrise:
    (a) normal front and rear position lights
    (b) additional front and rear position lamps fitted not more than 400 mm from the extreme edges of each side of the load
    (c) additional front and rear position lamps fitted anywhere on the load
    (d) additional red position lights to the rear

ENFORCEMENT OF MAINTENANCE STANDARDS

829. Which of the following officials is authorized to issue vehicle prohibition and defect notices?
    (a) an officer of HM Customs and Excise
    (b) a Trading Standards officer
    (c) a VOSA traffic examiner
    (d) a VOSA vehicle examiner

830. If a police officer in uniform stops a vehicle and issues the driver with a GV3 notice this is a direction:
    (a) to drive the vehicle to a place where it can be examined
    (b) to reduce the vehicle weight to within legal limits
    (c) to produce his driving licence at a police station within 7 days
    (d) preventing the vehicle being driven until it has been inspected

831. An immediate prohibition notice issued by a VOSA authorized vehicle examiner applies:
    (a) to the use of the vehicle for any purpose
    (b) to the use of the vehicle for specific purposes
    (c) to the use of the vehicle above a specified maximum speed
    (d) so as to prevent the carriage of goods on the vehicle

832. When a vehicle is found to have a defect that would not render it a danger to other road users, an authorized vehicle examiner would issue form:
    (a) PG9
    (b) PG9B
    (c) PG10
    (d) PGDN35

833. The official notice used by VOSA vehicle examiners to direct a vehicle to be taken to a specific place (not more than 5 miles away) for examination is form:
    (a) GV3
    (b) GV219
    (c) PG9B
    (d) GV160

834. A PG9 vehicle prohibition notice can be delayed before it takes effect up to a maximum of:
    (a) 5 days
    (b) 7 days
    (c) 10 days
    (d) 14 days

835. A haulier with no facilities of their own contracts with a local garage for the inspection and repair of their vehicles. If one of their vehicles on the road is subsequently found to have defects:
    (a) the TC will hold the haulier responsible for the defects
    (b) the TC will hold the garage responsible for the defects
    (c) both the garage and the haulier are liable to be prosecuted
    (d) the haulier can escape liability as they have a contract with the garage

836. A vehicle operator has an immediate right of appeal against the imposition of a prohibition notice by a VOSA vehicle examiner at a roadside check:
    (a) True
    (b) False

837. If a VOSA vehicle examiner refuses to remove a PG9 vehicle prohibition notice, the operator may appeal to:
    (a) the Road Haulage Association
    (b) the VOSA Area Manager
    (c) the Traffic Commissioner
    (d) a goods vehicle test station manager

838. When a PG9 immediate prohibition is issued for a vehicle defect, a form PG9B will usually also be issued to:
    (a) remove the prohibition
    (b) allow the vehicle to move under certain conditions
    (c) refuse permission for the vehicle to be removed
    (d) notify the operator to reduce the weight of the load

839. Following the imposition of a PG9 prohibition on a vehicle, repairs are carried out and it is presented for clearance. If the goods vehicle examiner imposes a GV9C this means:
    (a) the prohibition has been removed
    (b) the vehicle is still not roadworthy and the original prohibition remains in force
    (c) the vehicle can be driven away subject to certain conditions
    (d) only minor attention is still needed so the vehicle can be used

840. A goods vehicle subject to a PG9 prohibition by a VOSA vehicle examiner is re-submitted to a test station where form PG10 is issued. This means:
    (a) the examiner refuses to remove the prohibition
    (b) the defects are cleared and the prohibition has been removed
    (c) further defects are found and the prohibition remains in force
    (d) further defects are found and another prohibition is applied

841. A PG9 prohibition notice imposed on a goods vehicle can only be completely removed by the issue of form:
    (a) PG9A
    (b) PG9B
    (c) PG9C
    (d) PG10

842. Issue of a form PGDN (35) defect notice means:
    (a) that the vehicle has been inspected by a VOSA vehicle examiner
    (b) that the operator is to be prosecuted for maintenance offences
    (c) confirmation that a prohibition notice has been issued
    (d) the vehicle has defects which, in the interest of road safety, should be rectified

843. When a goods vehicle has been weighed at a roadside check and found to be within legal limits, a certificate of weight is issued exempting the vehicle from further weight checks
    (a) within the next 7 days
    (b) at VOSA weigh-stations during the next 24 hours
    (c) during the continuance of the same journey with the same load
    (d) before the vehicle returns to its authorized operating centre

844. If a goods vehicle is found at a VOSA roadside check to be loaded in excess of legal limits, the driver will be issued with a prohibition notice on form:
    (a) PG9
    (b) PG10
    (c) GV160
    (d) GV219

845. When an authorized examiner is refused permission to carry out vehicle inspections on an operator's premises, the examiner can exercise their powers to enter the premises for the purpose, provided they gives notice in writing:
    (a) at least 24 hours in advance
    (b) at least 36 hours in advance
    (c) at least 48 hours in advance
    (d) sent by recorded delivery at least 72 hours in advance

846. A police constable in uniform can instruct the driver of a stationary goods vehicle to take it to a place for inspection (without risk of claims) not more than:
    (a) 3 miles away
    (b) 5 miles away
    (c) 7 miles away
    (d) 10 miles away

847. An authorized vehicle examiner can legally divert a vehicle to a place for weighing or inspection (without risk of claims) for a distance not exceeding:
    (a) 1 mile
    (b) 2 miles
    (c) 5 miles
    (d) 7 miles

848. When a vehicle has been diverted by an authorized examiner to a weighbridge more than 5 miles distant and the weight is found to be within legal limits:
    (a) the operator has no claim for the delay to the journey
    (b) the operator can claim a standard mileage allowance from VOSA
    (c) a claim for expenses can be made to the highway authority
    (d) an appeal can be made to the Secretary of State for Transport

VEHICLE MAINTENANCE

849. When a haulier contracts out their vehicle service and repairs, the legal responsibility for keeping maintenance records rests with:
   (a) the operator
   (b) both the operator and the repair garage
   (c) neither the operator nor the repair garage
   (d) the repair garage

850. A transport operator must keep records of all defect inspections and repairs to their 'O' licensed vehicles and preserve them for at least:
   (a) 6 months
   (b) 9 months
   (c) 12 months
   (d) 15 months

851. If a transport operator has a proper maintenance agreement with a repair garage, then so far as their 'O' licence is concerned, responsibility for an unroadworthy vehicle rests with the repairer:
   (a) True
   (b) False

852. Traffic Commissioners require operators to have their vehicle maintenance inspections carried out at regular intervals of:
   (a) once every month
   (b) once every two months
   (c) 3,000–5,000 miles
   (d) no specified interval of time

SAFE LOADING OF VEHICLES AND TRANSIT OF GOODS

853. The legal requirement for the safe loading of vehicles is contained in the:
   (a) Goods Vehicles (Operators' Licences, Qualifications and Fees) Regulations 1984
   (b) Carriage of Goods by Road Act 1965
   (c) Goods Vehicles (Ascertainment of Maximum Gross Weights) Regulations 1976
   (d) Road Vehicles (Construction and Use) Regulations 1986

854. The 'Safety of Loads on Vehicles' Code of Practice states that rope used for load lashing should be at least:
    (a) 3-strand and minimum 10 mm nominal diameter
    (b) 3-strand and minimum 12 mm nominal diameter
    (c) 3-strand and minimum 15 mm nominal diameter
    (d) 5-strand and minimum 10 mm nominal diameter

855. The DOT Code of Practice on the safe loading of vehicles states that to prevent movement of the load in a forward direction, a load restraint device should be capable of withstanding a force equal to:
    (a) half the total weight of the load
    (b) three-quarters of the total weight of the load
    (c) the full weight of the load
    (d) twice the full weight of the load

856. The legal requirements on load safety are that vehicle operators must:
    (a) use only approved webbing straps and tensioners for securing loads
    (b) ensure that all loads are secure and not likely to cause danger
    (c) use only British Standards approved load-restraint systems
    (d) follow the guidelines in the Code of Practice on load safety

857. If a heavy goods vehicle is found by the police to be overloaded, prosecution and likely conviction for this offence will rest with:
    (a) the driver only
    (b) the driver's employer only
    (c) both the driver and their employer
    (d) the vehicle loaders

858. If a load shifts or falls from a heavy goods vehicle, who is liable to prosecution for an insecure load?
    (a) the driver only
    (b) the driver's employer
    (c) both the driver and their employer
    (d) the vehicle loaders

859. While travelling on a road, part of a load falls from a vehicle when a faulty rope breaks. What legal action will follow?
    (a) if the driver was not aware of the fault in the rope they are not liable
    (b) there is no defence against using a vehicle with an insecure load
    (c) liability rests with the loader, not the driver
    (d) as the rope breakage was accidental no offence has been committed

860. Which of the following vehicles can be driven across a half-barrier level crossing without first obtaining permission from the signalman?
(a) a vehicle exceeding 38 tonnes maximum permissible weight
(b) a vehicle exceeding 9 ft 6 in in width
(c) a vehicle exceeding 48 ft in length
(d) a vehicle incapable of exceeding 5 mph

TRANSPORT OPERATING SYSTEMS

861. The principal advantage of using the Kangourou road–rail system for international journeys through France is that it:
(a) dispenses with the need for TIR carnets
(b) dispenses with the need to operate under the CMR convention
(c) avoids the need for payment of deposits against Customs duties
(d) saves drivers having to worry about exceeding their driving hours en route through France

862. The Freight Shuttle through the Channel-Tunnel rail system is known as a:
(a) rolling motorway system
(b) multi-modal system
(c) piggyback system
(d) bi-lateral rail system

863. The Kombiverkher road–rail system operated by German Railways (DB) can be used for:
(a) complete vehicles only
(b) unaccompanied trailers only
(c) accompanied vehicles and unaccompanied trailers
(d) accompanied trailers and semi-trailers only

864. Road–rail certificates must be stamped by rail authorities as proof that:
(a) the vehicle/trailer has been carried on the train
(b) the necessary Customs clearances have been obtained en route
(c) an ATA carnet exists for temporary importation of the vehicle
(d) the vehicle/trailer and load are fully insured for CMR liabilities

865. Under which international convention are UK vehicles travelling abroad required to carry independently powered flashing lights?
    (a) AETR convention
    (b) CMR convention
    (c) ADR convention
    (d) AGR convention

ABNORMAL, LONG AND WIDE LOADS

866. A load 25.5 metres long may be carried on a standard vehicle provided that:
    (a) 2 days' notice is given to the police for every district through which it is to pass
    (b) a statutory attendant is carried
    (c) prior approval is obtained from the Secretary of State for Transport
    (d) legal requirements for the display of marker boards are observed

867. When moving abnormal indivisible loads, if the total weight of the vehicle and its load exceeds 80,000 kg the road and bridge authorities concerned must be given:
    (a) 2 clear working days' notice
    (b) 3 clear working days' notice
    (c) 5 clear working days' notice
    (d) 6 clear working days' notice

868. Five clear days' notice in prescribed form must be given to every road and bridge authority concerned where the gross weight of a loaded Special Types vehicle exceeds:
    (a) 50,000 kg
    (b) 60,000 kg
    (c) 80,000 kg
    (d) 150,000 kg

869. Special Types vehicles of category 1 carrying a load are restricted to a maximum speed on single-carriageway roads of:
    (a) 12 mph
    (b) 20 mph
    (c) 30 mph
    (d) 40 mph

870. The maximum permitted weight for a category 3 Special Types vehicle and load is:
    (a) 60 tonnes
    (b) 76.2 tonnes
    (c) 80 tonnes
    (d) 150 tonnes

871. Under the Special Types General Order (STGO) a statutory attendant must be carried when the width of a vehicle or its load exceeds:
    (a) 1.83 metres
    (b) 2.5 metres
    (c) 2.9 metres
    (d) 3.5 metres

872. Under the Special Types General Order special authorization from the Secretary of State for Transport is needed if the width of a vehicle and load exceeds:
    (a) 3.5 metres
    (b) 5.0 metres
    (c) 6.0 metres
    (d) 9.0 metres

873. Under the Special Types General Order an attendant must be carried when a vehicle and its load exceed an overall length of:
    (a) 15 metres
    (b) 16.8 metres
    (c) 18 metres
    (d) 18.3 metres

874. A statutory attendant must accompany a vehicle travelling under the Special Types General Order when:
    (a) the load projects 2 metres beyond the rear of the vehicle
    (b) the vehicle and load are 4 metres wide
    (c) the overall length of both vehicle and load is 15 metres
    (d) a load projects to the front by 1.5 metres

875. When five abnormal indivisible loads normally requiring statutory attendants travel in convoy, attendants should be carried on:
    (a) the first vehicle only
    (b) each alternate vehicle
    (c) the last vehicle only
    (d) the first and last vehicles in the convoy

876. Advance notice must be given to the police for each district when it is proposed to move a vehicle and load having a rearward projection exceeding:
    (a) 3.05 metres
    (b) 2.9 metres
    (c) 1.83 metres
    (d) 1.07 metres

877. A vehicle carrying a load which projects 1.50 metres beyond the front and 1.75 metres beyond the rear of the vehicle must be marked:
    (a) so as to make the rear projection clearly visible
    (b) with a front marker board only
    (c) with a rear marker board only
    (d) with both front and rear marker boards

878. Road vehicle C&U regulations require goods vehicles carrying loads projecting rearward in excess of 1.0 metre but not in excess of 2.0 metres to:
    (a) have the projection made clearly visible
    (b) display end and side marker boards
    (c) display end and side marker boards and carry an attendant
    (d) display end and side marker boards, carry an attendant and notify the police in advance

879. Marker boards used for indicating projecting loads must be:
    (a) indirectly illuminated at night
    (b) directly illuminated at night
    (c) made of red fluorescent material on a white background
    (d) made of red reflex reflecting material on a white background

880. Which of the following loads must be marked with side and end marker boards?
    (a) a load projecting 2 metres rearward
    (b) a load projecting 4 metres forward
    (c) a load projecting 1.7 metres forward
    (d) a load projecting 3 metres rearward

881. A vehicle with a load overhanging the rear by 1.9 metres requires:
    (a) at least 2 clear days' advance notice to the police
    (b) the projection to be made clearly visible
    (c) the speed of the vehicle to be restricted to 30 mph
    (d) a statutory attendant to be carried on the vehicle

882. Where a load projects beyond the front of the vehicle by 3.09 metres, the procedure should be to:
 (a) notify the police 2 days in advance
 (b) notify the police and carry a statutory attendant
 (c) notify the police, carry a statutory attendant and display side and end marker boards
 (d) notify the highway and bridge authorities

883. Regulations require that a goods vehicle carrying a load projecting rearward in excess of 2.0 metres but not in excess of 3.05 metres must have:
 (a) an end marker board only
 (b) both end and side marker boards
 (c) both end and side marker boards and carry an attendant
 (d) both end and side marker boards, carry an attendant, and advance notice must given to the police

884. A UK haulier taking an abnormal indivisible load to France will need authority from:
 (a) French Customs authorities
 (b) the French Department of Transport, Paris
 (c) the French Embassy in London
 (d) the police for each region in France through which the load will pass

CARRIAGE OF DANGEROUS GOODS

885. Which authority in the UK is responsible for making and enforcing the regulations relating to the carriage of dangerous substances by road?
 (a) the police
 (b) the Health and Safety Executive
 (c) the Department for Transport
 (d) the Department of Trade and Industry

886. The Carriage of Dangerous Goods (Classification, Packaging and Labelling) Regulations 1996 define a tank container as having a total capacity exceeding:
 (a) 250 litres
 (b) 400 litres
 (c) 450 litres
 (d) 1,000 litres

887. A haulier must be provided with information in writing when collecting a tanker load of dangerous goods covered by the ADR Dangerous Goods List. The information details the:
    (a) risks to health and safety created by the substance
    (b) name of the original manufacturer of the substance
    (c) location of safe parking areas en route
    (d) individual chemical constituents of the substance

888. Disapplication to ADR 2003 applies when carrying dangerous goods in transport category 3 if:
    (a) no more than 32 gallons is conveyed in metal drums
    (b) they are conveyed in containers not exceeding 5 litres
    (c) the total mass or volume does not exceed 1,000 litres
    (d) they are conveyed in containers not exceeding 250 litres

889. Information concerning a dangerous goods being carried by road is usually carried in the form of a Tremcard, which is a document to be:
    (a) carried on the vehicle at all times when it is loaded with dangerous goods
    (b) shown to the police for every district through which the vehicle passes
    (c) given to the Fire Brigade when called to deal with an emergency situation
    (d) produced by the driver as evidence of their dangerous goods training

890. Which of the following legal requirements do not generally have to be met when dangerous goods are carried by road?
    (a) a suitable and efficient fire extinguisher must be carried
    (b) employees must be made aware of and comply with appropriate regulations
    (c) details of movements must be advised to the police and highway authorities
    (d) steps must be taken to ensure that none of the substance is spilt

891. Road tankers carrying a flammable substance on a journey within the UK must display an approved flame symbol, which is:
    (a) red on a black background
    (b) black on a red background
    (c) black on a orange reflective background
    (d) luminous orange on a black matt background

892. A hazardous warning label displayed on a road tanker carrying a multi-load of dangerous goods must contain:
    (a) identification labels for all the substances carried
    (b) a list of all the individual substances carried
    (c) the word 'multi-load'
    (d) the names of the manufacturers of each of the substances

893. Hazardous warning notices on tanker vehicles show two sets of letters or numbers, the lower set with a 4-digit number being the substance identification number while the upper set is:
    (a) the emergency action code
    (b) the substance name or code number
    (c) a flammable symbol
    (d) an emergency contact telephone number

894. Road tankers carrying listed dangerous goods are required to display a rectangular warning notice giving details including the:
    (a) destination of the load
    (b) emergency service to be notified in case of accident
    (c) place where the vehicle was loaded
    (d) emergency action code for the particular substance

895. If a bulk road tanker carries dangerous goods between the UK and Germany what regulations apply?
    (a) British hazardous goods regulations
    (b) ATP Convention rules
    (c) AGR Convention rules
    (d) ADR and IMDG blue book rules

CARRIAGE OF FOOD

896. A food delivery driver who may need to carry meat carcasses must wear a hat so that the meat does not touch their hair.
    (a) True
    (b) False

CARRIAGE OF LIVE ANIMALS

897. The load compartment of a vehicle designed to carry animals must be:
    (a) suitably strengthened
    (b) lined with insulating material
    (c) lined with a washable surface
    (d) free from sharp projections

898. Horses may be transported in road vehicles for up to 24 hours if they are provided with:
    (a) a constant supply of feed and water
    (b) water every 12 hours
    (c) a short exercise every 12 hours
    (d) liquid during the journey and feed every eight hours

899. Farm animals of different species may be carried in the same vehicle provided they are separated by fixed partitions:
    (a) True
    (b) False

900. Records relating to the carriage of animals must be retained and be available for inspection for at least:
    (a) 3 weeks
    (b) 3 months
    (c) 6 months
    (d) 12 months

CHAPTER 11

Typical questions:
Road safety

(covering syllabus sections H1 to H4)

DRIVER LICENSING

901. Large-goods-vehicle driving entitlements are currently issued by:
    (a) the Traffic Commissioner at Traffic Area offices
    (b) the Driver and Vehicle Licensing Agency, Swansea
    (c) main post offices
    (d) local licensing offices

902. The Traffic Commissioner retains powers in respect of LGV driver:
    (a) applications and decisions
    (b) employment records
    (c) conduct and discipline
    (d) medical records

903. A medical certificate must accompany the first application for an LGV driving entitlement and all renewals made after the applicant reaches the age of:
    (a) 45 years
    (b) 60 years
    (c) 62 years
    (d) 65 years

904. Which of the following vehicles are exempt from the need for the driver to hold an LGV driving entitlement?
    (a) goods vehicles operating under a trade licence
    (b) public service vehicles
    (c) goods vehicles not exceeding 10 tonnes permissible maximum weight
    (d) articulated tractive units exceeding 3.05 tonnes unladen with no semi-trailer attached

905. An application for an LGV entitlement can be made ahead of the date required but not exceeding a period of:
    (a) 1 month
    (b) 2 months
    (c) 4 weeks
    (d) 3 months

906. LGV driving-entitlement applicants must declare any convictions for hours and records, loading and vehicle-roadworthiness offences during the:
    (a) past 4 years
    (b) past 5 years
    (c) past 7 years
    (d) past 10 years

907. For the purposes of driver licensing which of the following is classified as a 'small goods vehicle'?
    (a) a goods vehicle with a permissible maximum weight of 6.5 tonnes drawing a trailer of 2 tonnes
    (b) a goods vehicle with a permissible maximum weight of 7 tonnes drawing a trailer of 1 tonne
    (c) a goods vehicle with a permissible maximum weight of 7 tonnes drawing a trailer of 2 tonnes
    (d) a goods vehicle with a permissible maximum weight of 2.5 tonnes drawing a trailer of 1 tonne

908. A learner LGV driver holding both provisional LGV and ordinary entitlements must display on the front and rear of the vehicle:
    (a) an LGV 'L' plate only
    (b) either LGV or ordinary 'L' plates
    (c) an ordinary 'L' plate only
    (d) a driver training school plate

909. A learner can take the LGV driving test while holding both provisional ordinary and provisional LGV driving licences to obtain a certificate of competence to drive LGVs of the type on which the test was taken and vehicles of category B:
(a) True
(b) False

910. The holder of provisional category C driving entitlement must comply with which of the following conditions?
(a) they are not allowed to drive on a motorway
(b) they must be tested on a goods vehicle exceeding 7.5 tonnes
(c) they can drive a 4-wheel rigid vehicle towing a drawbar trailer
(d) they can drive an artic tractive unit with automatic transmission

911. When a broken-down heavy goods vehicle is being towed on a rigid towbar the person steering it must hold:
(a) a full category B driving entitlement
(b) an LGV driving entitlement of the appropriate class
(c) both an ordinary driving licence and a provisional LGV entitlement
(d) a driving licence is not needed for this purpose

912. If the driver of a large goods vehicle is taken ill while driving on a motorway and is unable to continue their journey:
(a) they must struggle on to the next service area to get help
(b) the vehicle may be driven to safety by a police officer even though the officer may not hold the correct LGV entitlement
(c) the vehicle owner must send a replacement driver to remove it
(d) it can only be moved by an AA/RAC patrolman with an LGV licence

913. In order to take the category C LGV driving test a person must hold:
(a) a provisional ordinary driving licence only
(b) a provisional LGV driving entitlement only
(c) a full category B and a provisional category C entitlement
(d) both a provisional or full ordinary driving licence and a provisional LGV driving licence

914. The minimum age at which a driver may drive an articulated vehicle (where the tractive unit exceeds 2 tonnes unladen) on the road is:
(a) 17 years
(b) 18 years
(c) 21 years
(d) 25 years

915. The minimum age at which a person can drive a goods vehicle with a permissible maximum weight of 3 tonnes is:
(a) 17 years
(b) 18 years
(c) 19 years
(d) 21 years

916. Where a goods vehicle exceeds 3.5 tonnes but not 7.5 tonnes permissible maximum weight the driver must be aged at least:
(a) 16 years
(b) 17 years
(c) 18 years
(d) 21 years

917. The holder of a category C LGV driving entitlement is limited to driving:
(a) rigid vehicles towing a single-axle trailer not over 750 kg MAM
(b) rigid vehicles only
(c) small goods vehicles and minibuses
(d) goods vehicles not exceeding 10 tonnes maximum weight

918. A category C LGV driver learning to drive vehicles of category C+E would need to be accompanied by the holder of a current LGV driving licence of:
(a) category B+E
(b) category D+E
(c) category C+E
(d) All groups

919. Where employee drivers hold LGV driving entitlements of category C+E, ideally replacement vehicles should be of which of the following types?
(a) articulated vehicles only
(b) drawbar combinations only
(c) either artics or drawbar combinations
(d) maximum-weight rigid vehicles

920. The holder of a category C+E LGV driving entitlement may drive a 2-axle articulated tractive unit with no trailer attached:
(a) True
(b) False

921. The holder of a category B driving entitlement is allowed to drive which of the following vehicles?
(a) a private car with a trailer of over 750 kg attached
(b) a van and trailer of 8.5 tonnes combined weight
(c) a 6 tonne van with a 2.5 tonne twin-axle boat-trailer attached
(d) a goods vehicle up to 7.6 tonnes permissible maximum weight

922. The holder of a category C1 driving entitlement may drive which of the following vehicles?
(a) a 12-seater hire-or-reward minibus
(b) any goods vehicle without a trailer attached
(c) a goods vehicle not over 7.5 tonnes with no trailer attached
(d) a goods vehicle not over 7.5 tonnes with any trailer attached

923. The holder of a category C entitlement may not drive which of the following vehicles?
(a) a goods vehicle with a 6-tonne single-axle trailer
(b) a goods vehicle with a two-axle one-tonne trailer
(c) a goods vehicle of 7.6 tonnes maximum weight
(d) a rigid 30-tonne 8-wheel tipper

924. When a Traffic Commissioner revokes an LGV driving entitlement the holder can appeal after giving notice to:
(a) the Secretary of State for Transport
(b) the Transport Tribunal
(c) a magistrates' court
(d) the High Court

925. A driver whose LGV driving licence has been suspended by a Traffic Commissioner can appeal against the decision to:
(a) a magistrates' court
(b) the County Court
(c) the Court of Appeal
(d) the Transport Tribunal

926. To which of the following persons is a driver legally required to produce their driving licence on demand?
(a) a goods vehicle examiner
(b) a lorry park attendant
(c) a Customs and Excise officer
(d) a person whose car they have damaged

927. If a Department for Transport authorized examiner demands production of a driver's licence, the law allows the driver to produce
it:
    (a) at a police station named by the driver within 5 days
    (b) at the office of the examiner or the Traffic Commissioner
        within 5 days
    (c) at the office of the examiner or the Traffic Commissioner
        within 10 days
    (d) at any nominated police station within 10 days

DRIVING OFFENCES AND PENALTIES

928. Which of the following offences, on conviction by a court, will
result in automatic endorsement of a driving licence?
    (a) using a vehicle without a valid test certificate
    (b) making a U-turn in a prohibited area
    (c) using a vehicle without insurance against third-party risks
    (d) causing an obstruction with a vehicle

929. A driver convicted of three driving-licence endorsable offences
committed on the same occasion and which carry 3, 4 and 5
penalty points respectively will have which of the following number of points endorsed on their driving licence?
    (a) 3 points
    (b) 5 points
    (c) 9 points
    (d) 12 points

930. Where 12 penalty points for offences committed within a 3-year
period have already been added to a licence and the driver has been
disqualified once previously during that period, unless they can put
forward mitigating circumstances acceptable to the court, they will
be disqualified for at least:
    (a) 3 years
    (b) 2 years
    (c) 1 year
    (d) 6 months

931. Which of the following motoring offences will result in discretionary driving-licence disqualification on conviction?
    (a) racing on the highway
    (b) causing death by reckless driving
    (c) failure to stop after an accident
    (d) driving while under the influence of drink or drugs

932. Unless the court accepts a plea of exceptional hardship, a first conviction for dangerous driving will result in:
   (a) obligatory disqualification
   (b) discretionary disqualification
   (c) endorsement of full penalty points
   (d) endorsement of 8–10 penalty points

933. Which of the following offences requires the court to impose an obligatory disqualification from driving unless there are acceptable grounds of exceptional hardship?
   (a) exceeding statutory speed limits
   (b) dangerous driving within three years of a similar conviction
   (c) being in charge of a vehicle while having an excessive breath/alcohol level
   (d) leaving a vehicle in a dangerous position

934. One of the offences which incurs obligatory disqualification of a driving licence on conviction is:
   (a) driving with uncorrected defective eyesight
   (b) failing to stop at a traffic signal
   (c) exceeding the speed limit
   (d) racing on the highway

935. Three of the offences listed below incur automatic disqualification from driving for a minimum of 12 months, unless the court accepts reasons of exceptional hardship. Which of the offences does not incur this penalty?
   (a) causing death by dangerous driving
   (b) a second dangerous-driving offence in a 3-year period
   (c) racing on a highway
   (d) being in charge of a motor vehicle while under the influence of drink or drugs

936. The minimum period of mandatory driving-licence disqualification for a second drink/driving offence committed within 10 years is:
   (a) 10 years
   (b) 11 years
   (c) 3 years
   (d) 5 years

937. A person who is disqualified from driving for more than 10 years may apply to the court to have their disqualification removed:
    (a) after 2 years from the date on which it was imposed
    (b) after half the period of disqualification has expired
    (c) after 5 years from the date of disqualification
    (d) at no time during the disqualification period

938. When an application for removal of a driving-licence disqualification is refused by the court, the applicant may re-apply at intervals of:
    (a) 1 month
    (b) 2 months
    (c) 3 months
    (d) 6 months

939. For which of the following offences committed by a driver would the vehicle user also be liable to prosecution and a penalty of driving licence endorsement or disqualification?
    (a) failing to comply with the conditions of a provisional licence
    (b) stealing a motor vehicle
    (c) use of a vehicle uninsured against third-party risks
    (d) illegally carrying a passenger on a motorcycle

940. If a driver is disqualified from driving, they automatically lose their LGV driving entitlement for the same period:
    (a) True
    (b) False

941. A driving licence will be endorsed if the driver is convicted of which of the following offences?
    (a) failing to comply with traffic directions
    (b) driving without statutory lights
    (c) sounding a horn during the hours of darkness
    (d) failing to use the vehicle reversing alarm

942. Driving-licence endorsements for driving with a breath/alcohol level above the statutory limit remain in force for:
    (a) 3 years
    (b) 4 years
    (c) 10 years
    (d) 11 years

943. Except in the case of certain drink/driving offences, a driving-licence endorsement remains in force for a period of:
 (a) 3 years
 (b) 4 years
 (c) 10 years
 (d) 11 years

944. If a driving licence was endorsed for a drink/driving offence on 1 September 2000, the earliest date on which an application can be made for its removal is:
 (a) 1 September 2001
 (b) 1 September 2003
 (c) 1 September 2010
 (d) 1 September 2011

945. A police constable in uniform can request a driver to take a breath test at the roadside if the officer had reason to suspect the driver of having committed a traffic offence:
 (a) True
 (b) False

946. For the purposes of the breathalyser test, the prescribed limit for a driver is:
 (a) 30 microgrammes of alcohol in 100 millilitres of breath
 (b) 35 microgrammes of alcohol in 100 millilitres of breath
 (c) 40 microgrammes of alcohol in 100 millilitres of breath
 (d) 50 microgrammes of alcohol in 100 millilitres of breath

947. Where a driver is found by the police to have a breath/alcohol level of 30 microgrammes of alcohol per 100 millilitres of breath, they are over the statutory limit and have committed an offence:
 (a) True
 (b) False

948. It is an offence to drive a motor vehicle on the road when the level of alcohol in the breath exceeds:
 (a) 20 microgrammes of alcohol per 80 millilitres of breath
 (b) 25 microgrammes of alcohol per 100 millilitres of breath
 (c) 35 microgrammes of alcohol per 100 millilitres of breath
 (d) 50 microgrammes of alcohol per 150 millilitres of breath

949. A person is liable to be convicted of an offence of driving with an excessive blood/alcohol level when this exceeds:
(a) 70 milligrammes of alcohol in 120 millilitres of blood
(b) 80 milligrammes of alcohol in 100 millilitres of blood
(c) 80 milligrammes of alcohol in 120 millilitres of blood
(d) 100 milligrammes of alcohol in 80 millilitres of blood

950. Where an employed driver is charged with not complying with vehicle insurance requirements, they have a valid defence if they can prove to the court that the vehicle did not belong to them and that they had no reason to believe it was not insured:
(a) True
(b) False

951. For which of the following offences could a goods-vehicle operator be convicted by a court even though they were not driving the vehicle at the time?
(a) failure of the driver to stop following an accident as required by law
(b) failure of the driver to comply with authorized traffic directions
(c) failure to hold insurance cover against third-party risks
(d) failure of the driver to give their name at the scene of an accident

952. The registered keeper of a vehicle would not be liable for payment of fixed penalty charges if they can prove that at the relevant time the vehicle was in the possession of another person without their consent:
(a) True
(b) False

953. Which of the following traffic offences can result in a fixed penalty?
(a) driving while uninsured against third-party risks
(b) driving carelessly
(c) causing damage to authorized traffic signs
(d) driving the wrong way in a one-way street

954. A fixed-penalty notice can be issued by a police constable or a traffic warden for the offence of:
(a) parking a vehicle on a road at night without lights
(b) careless driving
(c) driving when uninsured against third-party risks
(d) failure to sign a driving licence

955. Under the driving-licence penalty-points system, the number of points incurred for exceeding the speed limit is:
(a) 3 points
(b) 4 points
(c) 5 to 8 points at the discretion of the court
(d) 9 points

TRAFFIC REGULATIONS

956. On roads signposted as rural clearways, restrictions on stopping do not apply to goods vehicles loading or unloading:
(a) True
(b) False

957. On roads signposted as rural clearways, waiting restrictions apply for:
(a) 4 hours daily
(b) 8 hours daily
(c) 12 hours daily
(d) 24 hours daily

958. On roads signposted as urban clearways, stopping restrictions apply only:
(a) during morning and evening peak periods
(b) from 7.00 am to 7.00 pm on Mondays to Fridays only
(c) for 24 hours every day
(d) from 7.00 am to 7.00 pm every day

959. Drivers are prohibited from stopping in a zebra-crossing controlled area for which of the following reasons?
(a) to avoid an accident
(b) to give precedence to a pedestrian on the crossing
(c) to load or unload goods
(d) to make a right or left turn

960. A vehicle has precedence over pedestrians at a pelican crossing when the amber light is flashing:
(a) True
(b) False

961. Goods vehicles may stop in vacant parking meter bays, without payment, to load and unload for up to:
    (a) 10 minutes
    (b) 15 minutes
    (c) 20 minutes
    (d) 30 minutes

962. A driver who parks their vehicle on a pavement or roadside verge to load or unload commits an offence if:
    (a) it is parked with the prior permission of a police officer
    (b) it is left with the hazard warning flashers operating
    (c) the loading/unloading could not have been reasonably carried out otherwise
    (d) it is more than 7.5 tonnes permissible maximum weight

963. Goods vehicles not exceeding 1,525 kg unladen weight can be parked without lights at night, provided they are in a 30 mph speed limit area, are parked on the nearside of the road and not within:
    (a) 15 feet from a road junction
    (b) 10 metres from a road junction on either side
    (c) 10 yards from a road junction on either side
    (d) 15 yards from a road junction

964. A driver is prohibited from stopping their vehicle on the hard shoulder of a motorway:
    (a) when they are taken ill
    (b) to give assistance to another vehicle which has broken down
    (c) to allow them to take an official break
    (d) in the case of an accident

965. Vehicles with an operating weight exceeding 7.5 tonnes are allowed to use the right-hand lane of motorways:
    (a) only in exceptional circumstances
    (b) under no circumstances whatsoever
    (c) at any time when it is safe to do so
    (d) to pass another vehicle carrying a wide load

966. Rural clearways are indicated by signs comprising:
    (a) a circular plate with red border and diagonal cross on a blue background
    (b) a rectangular plate with black lettering on a yellow background
    (c) a circular plate with a white symbol on a blue background
    (d) an octagonal plate with white letters on a red background

967. On a road marked as an urban clearway, stopping is prohibited at specified times except for picking up or setting down passengers when the stop may last for up to:
(a) one minute
(b) two minutes
(c) four minutes
(d) five minutes

968. A circular road sign bordered in red and showing a black silhouette of a vehicle and the symbol '7.5 T' means that goods vehicles:
(a) exceeding 7.5 tonnes unladen may pass
(b) exceeding 7.5 tonnes gross weight are prohibited
(c) not exceeding 7.5 tonnes unladen may pass
(d) not exceeding 7.5 tonnes gross weight are prohibited

969. A single continuous yellow line painted on the road parallel to the kerb means:
(a) waiting is prohibited at peak hours
(b) waiting is prohibited at any time
(c) waiting is prohibited during the times shown on the sign
(d) waiting is prohibited at any time during the working day

970. A double yellow line painted on the road parallel to the kerb means:
(a) loading/unloading is prohibited during every working day
(b) loading/unloading is prohibited at any other times as shown on the nearby sign
(c) waiting is prohibited at any time
(d) waiting is prohibited during any other period as shown on the nearby sign

971. A waiting prohibition that applies during every working day is indicated on a sign, which shows when the restriction applies, and is further indicated by:
(a) a single continuous-yellow line painted parallel to the kerb
(b) a single broken-yellow line painted parallel to the kerb
(c) a double-yellow line painted parallel to the kerb
(d) double-yellow lines painted on the kerb at right angles to the road

972. A single-yellow line painted on the kerb edging at right angles to the road means:
    (a) waiting is prohibited during every working day
    (b) waiting is prohibited during any other periods
    (c) loading/unloading is prohibited during every working day
    (d) loading/unloading is prohibited during the times shown on the nearby plate

973. A double-yellow line painted on the kerb edging at right angles to the road means that loading and unloading is prohibited:
    (a) at any time
    (b) during peak hours on working days only
    (c) during 24 hours every day
    (d) during the hours of darkness only

974. Yellow cross-hatched lines painted on the road mean:
    (a) loading/unloading is prohibited during every working day
    (b) loading/unloading is prohibited during every working day and at other times
    (c) a box junction on which you must not stop unless turning right
    (d) waiting is prohibited during the working day and at other times

975. It is illegal for vehicles other than buses to use bus lanes:
    (a) only on normal working days
    (b) during morning and evening peak periods
    (c) on any day when buses are operating
    (d) during times when the lanes are in operation (as indicated on a nearby sign)

976. Although no restrictions on loading and unloading are signposted, a police constable may still direct a driver to move their vehicle if it causes an obstruction:
    (a) True
    (b) False

977. A police constable in uniform or a vehicle examiner can direct a driver of a goods vehicle to take it to a place for inspection or weighing without risk of a claim for expenses, providing the distance does not exceed:
    (a) 3 miles
    (b) 4 miles
    (c) 5 miles
    (d) 10 miles

978. Traffic wardens are appointed by:
    (a) the area Traffic Commissioner
    (b) the local authority
    (c) the local police authority
    (d) the Secretary of State for Transport

979. Which of the following offences are not within a traffic warden's power to take action?
    (a) driving without a current or valid driving licence
    (b) causing an obstruction or contravening waiting restrictions
    (c) parking a vehicle at night without lights
    (d) failing to display a current vehicle excise licence disc

980. Persons employed as parking attendants by the local highway authority have duties in connection with:
    (a) school crossing patrols
    (b) the use of parking bays
    (c) the fixed-penalty system
    (d) point duties for traffic control

981. If a traffic warden believes a person to be the driver of a vehicle illegally parked without lights, they have the power to require that person to:
    (a) provide their name and address
    (b) produce their driving licence
    (c) produce a test certificate for the vehicle
    (d) produce evidence of insurance for the vehicle

982. Traffic wardens have power to enforce the law in connection with offences concerning:
    (a) stealing motor vehicles
    (b) failing to stop following a road accident
    (c) driving a vehicle with defective tyres
    (d) leaving a vehicle parked at night without lights

983. Excess parking charges are normally payable within:
    (a) 14 days of the issue of the notice
    (b) 21 days of the issue of the notice
    (c) 28 days of the issue of the notice
    (d) the time period stated in the notice

984. Under the fixed-penalty system, if the offending driver does not elect to have the case dealt with by a court, they must pay the penalty within:
(a) 7 days
(b) 14 days
(c) 21 days
(d) 28 days

985. If a fixed penalty has not been paid within the statutory period, within what period of time must the police contact the registered keeper of the vehicle for a statutory statement of ownership?
(a) 21 days
(b) 3 months
(c) 4 months
(d) 6 months

986. Which of the following countries imposes a Sunday driving ban on certain goods vehicles over 3.5 tonnes?
(a) Austria
(b) Germany
(c) Spain
(d) France

987. Which of the following countries imposes a night-time ban on the movement of goods vehicles on their roads?
(a) Denmark
(b) France
(c) Austria
(d) Italy

988. Which of the following countries bans goods vehicles over 7.5 tonnes laden weight from using motorways between 07.00 hrs on Saturday and 22.00 hrs on Sunday during the months of June to September?
(a) Germany
(b) Croatia
(c) Austria
(d) Greece

989. Which of the following countries bans the transit of heavy goods vehicles on Sunday?
(a) Norway
(b) Switzerland
(c) Sweden
(d) Finland

990. Which of the following countries bans the carriage of dangerous goods on its roads during all or part of the weekend?
(a) Norway
(b) France
(c) Portugal
(d) Belgium

991. It is compulsory for goods vehicles over 3.5 tonnes to carry wheel chocks in Austria:
(a) True
(b) False

992. A European Accident Statement:
(a) is required by the gendarmerie of EU states in which a road accident occurs
(b) assists insurance companies to deal more efficiently with claims arising from motor accidents in Europe
(c) must be completed by all UK drivers involved in accidents abroad
(d) ensures that blame for road accidents in Europe can be readily established

993. The AGR convention establishes:
(a) a European system for numbering road networks
(b) a system for control of the carriage of hazardous goods
(c) standard conditions of carriage for international journeys
(d) a system for controlling bilateral road haulage permit quotas

SPEED LIMITS

994. A 'restricted' road is a road in a built-up area where, usually, a 30 mph speed limit applies and where the street lamps are not more than:
(a) 100 feet apart
(b) 100 yards apart
(c) 200 feet apart
(d) 200 yards apart

995. Vehicles used by the emergency services are exempt from speed limits at all times:
(a) True
(b) False

996. When a vehicle subject to a specific speed limit is driven on a section of road where a different speed limit applies, the maximum speed at which it should be driven is:
(a) the lower limit applicable to the vehicle
(b) the lower limit applicable to the road
(c) the higher limit applicable to the vehicle
(d) the lower limit applicable to either the road or the vehicle

997. The general speed limit on derestricted roads other than motorways and dual-carriageway roads is:
(a) 40 mph
(b) 50 mph
(c) 60 mph
(d) 70 mph

998. Unless a lower speed limit applies, the maximum permitted speed for a motor vehicle on a dual carriageway is:
(a) 70 mph
(b) 60 mph
(c) 50 mph
(d) 40 mph

999. On motorways, dual-purpose vehicles are limited to a maximum speed of:
(a) 40 mph
(b) 50 mph
(c) 60 mph
(d) 70 mph

1000. The maximum permitted speed for a goods vehicle not exceeding 7.5 tonnes mlw and drawing a trailer is:
(a) 60 mph
(b) 50 mph
(c) 40 mph
(d) 30 mph

1001. The maximum permitted speed for a van with a gross weight of 3,550 kg on a single-carriageway road is:
(a) 30 mph
(b) 40 mph
(c) 50 mph
(d) 60 mph

1002. The maximum permitted speed for a van with an unladen weight of 1,200 kg on a single-carriageway road is:
(a) 30 mph
(b) 40 mph
(c) 50 mph
(d) 60 mph

1003. A rigid goods vehicle not exceeding 7,500 kg mlw may travel on motorways at a maximum speed of:
(a) 70 mph
(b) 60 mph
(c) 50 mph
(d) 40 mph

1004. The speed limit for a vehicle with a maximum laden weight not exceeding 7.5 tonnes and towing a trailer on a dual-carriageway road is:
(a) 30 mph
(b) 40 mph
(c) 50 mph
(d) 60 mph

1005. Which of the following categories of vehicle is restricted to 60 mph on motorways?
(a) rigid goods vehicles over 7.5 tonnes mlw
(b) vehicles designed to carry not more than 8 passengers
(c) dual-purpose vehicles
(d) rigid goods vehicles not exceeding 1,525 kg unladen

1006. The maximum permitted speed on a motorway for a goods vehicle with a maximum laden weight of 12,000 kg and towing a drawbar trailer is:
(a) 30 mph
(b) 40 mph
(c) 50 mph
(d) 60 mph

1007. The maximum permitted speed on a dual carriageway for a rigid 8-wheel vehicle is:
(a) 30 mph
(b) 40 mph
(c) 50 mph
(d) 60 mph

1008. The maximum permitted speed for an articulated vehicle exceeding 7.5 tonnes maximum laden weight on an ordinary derestricted road is:
(a) 30 mph
(b) 40 mph
(c) 50 mph
(d) 60 mph

1009. Works trucks are restricted to a maximum speed of:
(a) 18 mph
(b) 15 mph
(c) 20 mph
(d) 30 mph

1010. Special Types vehicles of Category III carrying a load are restricted to a maximum speed on motorways of:
(a) 12 mph
(b) 15 mph
(c) 20 mph
(d) 30 mph

SAFE WORKING PRACTICES

1011. The Freight Containers (Safety Convention) Regulations 1984 require safety-approval plates for freight containers to be issued by:
(a) the Health and Safety Executive (or a body appointed by the HSE)
(b) the Freight Transport Association
(c) VOSA Goods Vehicle Test Stations
(d) the British Safety Council

ROAD-TRAFFIC ACCIDENTS

1012. In which of the following accidents involving injury to animals must the driver stop and give particulars to the police or other persons with reasonable grounds for requiring them?
(a) where there is injury to a deer
(b) where there is injury to a pig carried in the vehicle
(c) where there is injury to a goat
(d) where there is injury to a goose

1013. The driver of a motor vehicle involved in a road accident is required by law to:
  (a) obtain the assistance of a police officer
  (b) place warning triangles on the road near the accident scene
  (c) stop and give particulars to any person reasonably requiring them
  (d) take adequate steps to protect people from further risks

1014. If a driver was not aware at the time that their vehicle had been involved in an accident, they may not be convicted for failing to stop and report it:
  (a) True
  (b) False

1015. If after stopping at an injury accident in which they are involved, the driver does not give necessary information to a police officer or other person having reasonable grounds for requiring it, they must report to the police:
  (a) within 24 hours
  (b) as soon as possible but in any case not later than 24 hours afterwards
  (c) within 5 days
  (d) immediately

1016. Road accidents should normally be reported to the vehicle insurers:
  (a) only if a claim is to be made
  (b) at the earliest opportunity
  (c) within 24 hours
  (d) within 7 days

1017. When involved in a personal-injury accident where the police take details at the scene, the driver is not required at that time to:
  (a) give their name and address
  (b) give the vehicle owner's name and address
  (c) give the vehicle registration number
  (d) produce the vehicle insurance certificate

1018. Following a road accident the term 'third party' refers to:
  (a) the insurance company
  (b) the other party involved
  (c) the owner of the vehicle
  (d) an eye-witness

1019. A motor-vehicle owner who was not driving at the time their vehicle was involved in a road accident:
    (a) must tell the police who was the driver if prosecution is intended for a road-traffic offence
    (b) must tell the police who was the driver if there was personal injury
    (c) must in any case tell the police the driver's identity if known
    (d) has no legal liability to tell the police who was the driver

1020. At the scene of a road accident where there are no personal injuries a driver is required by law to:
    (a) give details from their driving licence
    (b) produce their insurance policy for examination
    (c) give the serial number of their certificate of insurance to any witness
    (d) give their name and address to any person reasonably requiring it

1021. A driver has a legal responsibility to stop at the scene of a road accident:
    (a) if they run over a chicken
    (b) if they run over a stray cat
    (c) if they injure only themselves in the accident
    (d) if they injure a dog

1022. If legally required information was not given at the scene of a road accident involving personal injury or damage, this must be reported to the police by:
    (a) the driver by telephone
    (b) the driver in writing
    (c) a witness
    (d) the driver in person

1023. Which of the following constitutes a legally reportable road traffic accident?
    (a) where only the driver of the vehicle involved is injured
    (b) where sheep being carried on the vehicle involved are injured
    (c) where a passenger being carried in the vehicle involved is injured
    (d) where the driver of a vehicle knocks down and kills a cat

1024. What information must a driver involved in a road-traffic accident give to the driver of any other vehicle involved?
(a) his or her destination
(b) details from their driving licence
(c) the name and address of the vehicle owner
(d) the name and address of the vehicle owner's insurance company

1025. Under the Road Traffic Act 1988, section 170, which of the following constitutes a reportable road-traffic accident?
(a) running over and killing a goose
(b) colliding with another vehicle but causing no damage
(c) colliding with and damaging a wooden fence adjacent to the road
(d) the driver accidentally trapping a passenger's hand in the door

1026. If a lorry collides with a stationary car, damaging it but causing no personal injury, and the lorry driver, although aware of the accident, does not stop at the scene but reports the matter to the police two hours later:
(a) they commit no offence because the accident was reported to the police within 24 hours
(b) they commit an offence because they did not stop at the scene of the accident
(c) they do not commit an offence because no person was injured
(d) they commit no offence because the car was parked illegally blocking a delivery entrance

Answers to multiple-choice questions

Q	A	Q	A	Q	A	Q	A
1	c	21	d	41	c	61	c
2	b	22	b	42	a	62	d
3	c	23	a	43	b	63	c
4	c	24	d	44	c	64	a
5	b	25	c	45	c	65	b
6	d	26	a	46	a	66	b
7	d	27	a	47	c	67	b
8	d	28	c	48	c	68	a
9	c	29	d	49	a	69	d
10	b	30	a	50	c	70	c
11	b	31	a	51	a	71	c
12	a	32	c	52	b	72	c
13	d	33	d	53	b	73	a
14	b	34	b	54	b	74	c
15	a	35	c	55	a	75	a
16	b	36	d	56	d	76	c
17	d	37	d	57	d	77	a
18	a	38	d	58	c	78	c
19	c	39	c	59	d	79	a
20	b	40	b	60	a	80	b

Q	A	Q	A	Q	A	Q	A
81	a	115	b	149	c	183	b
82	c	116	d	150	d	184	b
83	c	117	b	151	b	185	c
84	a	118	c	152	c	186	b
85	d	119	a	153	d	187	b
86	b	120	b	154	b	188	c
87	c	121	a	155	c	189	a
88	a	122	c	156	b	190	b
89	b	123	c	157	c	191	d
90	c	124	c	158	b	192	a
91	b	125	a	159	c	193	a
92	a	126	c	160	b	194	d
93	b	127	a	161	d	195	c
94	b	128	d	162	c	196	c
95	c	129	c	163	a	197	b
96	a	130	c	164	b	198	d
97	c	131	c	165	c	199	b
98	a	132	a	166	d	200	d
99	b	133	c	167	b	201	c
100	b	134	d	168	b	202	c
101	a	135	a	169	d	203	b
102	d	136	c	170	b	204	c
103	d	137	c	171	a	205	b
104	a	138	c	172	b	206	d
105	c	139	d	173	d	207	b
106	c	140	a	174	c	208	b
107	d	141	c	175	b	209	d
108	d	142	a	176	c	210	d
109	a	143	c	177	d	211	b
110	d	144	d	178	c	212	c
111	b	145	c	179	c	213	c
112	a	146	c	180	b	214	d
113	c	147	d	181	c	215	d
114	c	148	c	182	d	216	d

Q	A	Q	A	Q	A	Q	A
217	c	251	a	285	d	319	d
218	d	252	a	286	a	320	c
219	a	253	b	287	b	321	c
220	b	254	a	288	c	322	b
221	c	255	a	289	a	323	b
222	a	256	c	290	d	324	c
223	c	257	b	291	c	325	b
224	a	258	b	292	c	326	b
225	d	259	b	293	b	327	a
226	c	260	c	294	b	328	a
227	d	261	b	295	b	329	b
228	a	262	c	296	d	330	b
229	c	263	d	297	d	331	c
230	d	264	a	298	a	332	a
231	a	265	d	299	c	333	a
232	a	266	b	300	d	334	a
233	c	267	c	301	b	335	d
234	d	268	d	302	d	336	d
235	b	269	b	303	c	337	c
236	a	270	b	304	b	338	c
237	d	271	b	305	d	339	b
238	c	272	d	306	d	340	b
239	c	273	a	307	c	341	a
240	a	274	b	308	a	342	b
241	c	275	d	309	d	343	a
242	d	276	a	310	a	344	a
243	c	277	b	311	b	345	d
244	b	278	b	312	d	346	a
245	a	279	b	313	c	347	a
246	d	280	c	314	a	348	c
247	b	281	c	315	b	349	c
248	c	282	c	316	c	350	c
249	a	283	b	317	d	351	c
250	b	284	a	318	d	352	d

Q	A	Q	A	Q	A	Q	A
353	b	387	c	421	a	455	b
354	d	388	b	422	c	456	c
355	a	389	a	423	b	457	a
356	d	390	d	424	b	458	c
357	a	391	b	425	b	459	a
358	d	392	d	426	b	460	d
359	d	393	c	427	c	461	d
360	d	394	b	428	c	462	a
361	a	395	a	429	b	463	a
362	b	396	b	430	a	464	a
363	c	397	a	431	d	465	c
364	c	398	c	432	c	466	b
365	d	399	b	433	d	467	b
366	a	400	d	434	b	468	a
367	d	401	d	435	b	469	c
368	c	402	c	436	b	470	d
369	b	403	a	437	a	471	b
370	d	404	a	438	a	472	d
371	a	405	b	439	c	473	a
372	a	406	c	440	d	474	a
373	d	407	d	441	c	475	c
374	a	408	b	442	a	476	d
375	b	409	a	443	b	477	d
376	c	410	a	444	d	478	d
377	d	411	d	445	b	479	b
378	d	412	b	446	d	480	b
379	d	413	b	447	b	481	d
380	a	414	b	448	c	482	b
381	c	415	b	449	b	483	c
382	c	416	b	450	b	484	b
383	d	417	c	451	c	485	c
384	d	418	c	452	d	486	a
385	a	419	a	453	b	487	d
386	b	420	b	454	b	488	a

Q	A	Q	A	Q	A	Q	A
489	b	523	a	557	d	591	a
490	d	524	d	558	d	592	b
491	c	525	d	559	d	593	b
492	b	526	b	560	c	594	c
493	c	527	a	561	c	595	c
494	b	528	a	562	d	596	c
495	d	529	a	563	c	597	c
496	a	530	a	564	c	598	b
497	d	531	a	565	a	599	b
498	c	532	d	566	b	600	d
499	d	533	b	567	b	601	b
500	d	534	a	568	d	602	c
501	a	535	b	569	d	603	d
502	a	536	a	570	d	604	b
503	a	537	d	571	b	605	b
504	a	538	d	572	b	606	d
505	a	539	a	573	c	607	a
506	d	540	d	574	c	608	a
507	b	541	a	575	d	609	a
508	b	542	b	576	a	610	a
509	c	543	b	577	b	611	b
510	c	544	d	578	c	612	c
511	c	545	b	579	d	613	a
512	a	546	b	580	a	614	a
513	c	547	a	581	d	615	a
514	a	548	a	582	d	616	c
515	c	549	b	583	c	617	c
516	c	550	d	584	c	618	b
517	c	551	c	585	d	619	d
518	d	552	c	586	a	620	b
519	d	553	c	587	a	621	b
520	b	554	d	588	c	622	a
521	c	555	c	589	c	623	a
522	b	556	c	590	b	624	b

Q	A	Q	A	Q	A	Q	A
625	d	659	a	693	d	727	c
626	c	660	c	694	d	728	b
627	b	661	c	695	c	729	b
628	d	662	a	696	b	730	d
629	a	663	c	697	d	731	d
630	d	664	b	698	c	732	b
631	a	665	c	699	b	733	c
632	d	666	a	700	d	734	b
633	c	667	c	701	a	735	d
634	a	668	d	702	d	736	a
635	d	669	a	703	b	737	a
636	a	670	c	704	b	738	d
637	d	671	d	705	b	739	a
638	b	672	a	706	b	740	b
639	b	673	a	707	c	741	c
640	c	674	b	708	c	742	a
641	b	675	b	709	a	743	b
642	d	676	d	710	d	744	c
643	c	677	a	711	c	745	b
644	a	678	b	712	c	746	b
645	b	679	d	713	d	747	c
646	c	680	b	714	c	748	a
647	a	681	a	715	c	749	c
648	a	682	c	716	d	750	c
649	a	683	a	717	c	751	b
650	b	684	d	718	c	752	d
651	c	685	a	719	d	753	a
652	a	686	b	720	a	754	c
653	a	687	d	721	c	755	a
654	b	688	a	722	b	756	d
655	a	689	a	723	b	757	a
656	a	690	a	724	c	758	c
657	c	691	d	725	c	759	a
658	c	692	b	726	a	760	d

Q	A	Q	A	Q	A	Q	A
761	a	795	b	829	d	863	c
762	d	796	c	830	a	864	a
763	c	797	d	831	a	865	c
764	a	798	a	832	d	866	d
765	c	799	b	833	a	867	c
766	d	800	c	834	c	868	c
767	d	801	d	835	a	869	d
768	c	802	a	836	b	870	d
769	d	803	a	837	b	871	d
770	c	804	c	838	b	872	b
771	c	805	a	839	b	873	d
772	c	806	d	840	b	874	b
773	a	807	c	841	d	875	d
774	c	808	b	842	d	876	a
775	c	809	b	843	c	877	a
776	d	810	a	844	c	878	a
777	b	811	c	845	d	879	a
778	a	812	b	846	b	880	b
779	a	813	b	847	c	881	b
780	d	814	a	848	c	882	c
781	b	815	c	849	a	883	a
782	d	816	c	850	d	884	d
783	c	817	a	851	b	885	c
784	d	818	b	852	d	886	c
785	a	819	d	853	d	887	a
786	b	820	d	854	a	888	c
787	c	821	c	855	c	889	a
788	b	822	d	856	b	890	c
789	d	823	c	857	c	891	b
790	b	824	d	858	c	892	c
791	a	825	c	859	b	893	a
792	c	826	c	860	c	894	d
793	c	827	d	861	d	895	d
794	b	828	b	862	a	896	a

Q	A	Q	A	Q	A	Q	A
897	d	930	c	963	b	996	d
898	d	931	c	964	c	997	c
899	a	932	b	965	d	998	a
900	c	933	b	966	a	999	d
901	b	934	d	967	b	1000	a
902	c	935	d	968	b	1001	c
903	a	936	c	969	c	1002	d
904	b	937	c	970	c	1003	a
905	d	938	d	971	a	1004	d
906	a	939	c	972	d	1005	a
907	d	940	a	973	a	1006	d
908	c	941	a	974	c	1007	c
909	b	942	d	975	d	1008	b
910	b	943	b	976	a	1009	a
911	b	944	d	977	c	1010	d
912	b	945	a	978	c	1011	a
913	c	946	b	979	a	1012	c
914	c	947	b	980	b	1013	c
915	a	948	c	981	a	1014	a
916	c	949	b	982	d	1015	b
917	a	950	a	983	d	1016	d
918	c	951	c	984	d	1017	d
919	c	952	a	985	d	1018	b
920	a	953	d	986	c	1019	a
921	a	954	a	987	c	1020	d
922	c	955	a	988	a	1021	d
923	a	956	b	989	b	1022	d
924	a	957	d	990	b	1023	c
925	a	958	a	991	a	1024	c
926	a	959	c	992	b	1025	c
927	c	960	b	993	a	1026	b
928	c	961	c	994	d		
929	b	962	d	995	b		

OCR sample case studies: Questions and answers

The following case-study scenarios and specimen answers are taken from OCR's specimen papers, for use of which acknowledgement is hereby given.

Author's advice

The author advises examination candidates to read both the scenario (ie the story) and the case-study examination paper very carefully. It is important to determine precisely what answers the examiner is looking for and not to waste valuable time giving information that is not required. Don't spend time writing long, essay-type answers: stick to presenting the facts, giving as many as possible, and where appropriate qualify those facts with a *brief* explanation. Marks are given for the inclusion of key facts, not for waffle, and if the question carries, say, five marks, try to include at least five key facts in your answer.

After each question are listed the specimen marks allocated by OCR to that question, with the points that the examiner would typically expect you to cover in your answer. These are only the topics expected, not necessarily the actual or complete answers required: the examiner would expect you to be more specific. For example, in the National scenario, Question 2 (a) and (b), the examiner would expect the candidate, at the least, to:

- state the legal requirement for the return of tachograph charts (ie within 21 days);
- outline a system for checking charts for legal compliance (eg check all charts received for: (a) correct completion of centre field: ie dates, vehicle no., odometer entries, etc; (b) compliance with the hours law: ie continuous driving, total daily and weekly driving, breaks, daily and weekly rest, etc; (c) other requirements: evidence of speeding, missing entries, interrupted recordings, etc);
- list the records which must be made and retained (eg driver defect reports, vehicle inspection and service records, etc – for 15 months);
- state what disciplinary procedures may be applied;
- outline the incentives that might be applied to encourage legal compliance;
- refer to the VOSA Guide to Maintaining Roadworthiness Code of Practice.

And in Question 3, note that – besides the relevant figures that must be stated – the examiner is expecting a statement about the financial situation of the company (it would be easy to forget to include this after working out the figures, and yet this part of the answer alone carries a possible 5 marks).

In the examinations candidates may use:

- diagrams wherever they will help to answer a question;
- a non-programmable calculator;
- a dictionary.

NATIONAL SCENARIO

Red Transport Ltd

You are the transport manager for Red Transport Ltd. The company was formed 16 years ago and has grown very rapidly during this time. It is involved in the transport of general cargo and some consignments of dangerous goods.

Red Transport Ltd currently operates from six depots nationwide. All depots have rigid vehicles and also articulated tractor units, which operate with trailers exceeding 1020 kg.

In the last few weeks you have carried out work for a new customer, ABC Imports Ltd, collecting cargo from sea-ports. This cargo arrives by sea in unaccompanied trailers. These are collected from the port by Red Transport Ltd.

VEHICLES

All vehicles operate six days per week with the exception of bank holiday weeks when they work four days. The company operates the following vehicles:

No. of vehicles	Type	Average quarterly mileage	Average mpg
15	7.5-tonne rigid box vehicles	15,600	17
10	17-tonne rigid box vehicles	23,400	12
5	17-tonne rigid refrigerated box vehicles	23,400	11
10	2 x 4 articulated tractor units	31,200	8
	tandem-axle trailers	24,000	
	tri-axle trailers	34,000	

STAFF

The following staff are employed:

- 1 managing director
- 1 sales manager
- 1 accountant
- 2 administrators
- 2 salespersons
- 1 transport manager
- 1 warehouse manager
- 1 traffic supervisor
- 35 drivers
- 3 traffic clerks
- 6 warehouse operatives

ACCOUNTS INFORMATION

The current cost of fuel is £3.25 per gallon. The company does not expect the cost of fuel to increase over the next three months.

Accounting periods for the company are four weeks in the first two months of a quarter and five weeks in the last month of the quarter.

Red Transport Ltd
Balance Sheet Information
as at 31 December 1998

	£
FIXED ASSETS	
Freehold property	250,000
Vehicles	1,765,000
Office furniture and equipment	60,000
Plant and equipment	190,000
CURRENT ASSETS	
Debtors	150,000
Stock	52,000
Cash	2,000
CURRENT LIABILITIES	
Tax	25,000
Bank overdraft	1,000
Creditors	74,000
LONG-TERM LIABILITIES	
Revenue reserves	180,000
Shares issued	2,500,000
Bank loans	400,000
Debentures	185,000

Red Transport Ltd
Trading Account Information
12 months to 31 December 1998

	£
Sales and haulage work done	1,880,000
Warehouse and rent receipts	610,000
Vehicle running costs	748,000
Vehicle hire	20,000
Subcontractors	2,000
Depreciation of vehicles	317,000
Insurance	80,000
Excise duty	100,000
Operator's licences	2,000
Operating wages	525,000

Red Transport Ltd
Profit-and-Loss Account Information
12 months to 31 December 1998

	£
Gross Profit	to be calculated
Less expenses:	
Directors' remunerations	90,000
Office salaries	190,000
Rates	17,000
Utilities	16,000
Telephone and postage	5,000
Interest charges on loans	48,000
Auditors' fees	14,000
Sundry expenses	26,000

CALENDAR EXTRACT

MONTH 1

M	T	W	T	F	S	S
1*	2	3	4	5	6	7
8	9	10	11	12	13	14
15	16	17	18	19	20	21
22*	23	24	25	26	27	28
29	30	31				

MONTH 2

M	T	W	T	F	S	S
			1	2	3	4
5	6	7	8	9	10	11
12	13	14	15	16	17	18
19	20	21	22	23	24	25
26*	27	28	29	30		

MONTH 3

M	T	W	T	F	S	S
					1	2
3	4	5	6	7	8	9
10	11	12	13	14	15	16
17	18	19	20	21	22	23
24	25	26	27	28	29	30

*Bank Holiday

CASE-STUDY QUESTIONS

Read the Case-Study Scenario and answer ALL questions.

1. Your customer ABC Imports Ltd has sent you a claim for damage to their goods whilst they were in your possession. Red's managing director asked you what rules are likely to apply to the liability of the company. Explain the possible liabilities Red Transport Ltd could have in these circumstances. (10 marks)

OCR specimen marks:
- Knowledge that they may be liable to CMR (1 mark)
- and reason (3 marks)
- SDRs 8.33 (2 marks)
- From date goods accepted for carriage (1 mark)
- Liability does not exceed value of goods (1 mark)
- Time limits (1 mark)
- Mention of identification of defences (1 mark)

---

2. (a) Explain how you control and monitor legally required transport-related documents in relation to vehicles and drivers to ensure that Red Transport Ltd complies with the regulations and laws relating to them. (10 marks)

OCR specimen marks:
- Issue and return of tachographs (1 mark)
- Viability of control (4 marks)
- Filing system for vehicle records (1 mark)
- Records to be filed (3 marks)
- Checking method (1 mark)

   (b) You noticed from returned tachograph charts that one of your drivers, Fred Green, who has been employed for 10 years by the company, consistently breaks transport regulations and has a poor accident record. Explain how you would deal with this? (5 marks)

OCR specimen marks:
- Disciplinary action (1 mark)
- Incentives (1 mark)
- Code of practice (3 marks)

---

3. (a) From the Accounts information in the Scenario, calculate the following:
   – capital employed
   – percentage of direct costs compared to turnover
   – the return on capital employed.
   (b) Explain what the financial situation of the company is after assessing the acid-test ratio (15 marks)

OCR specimen marks:

(a) – Capital employed: fixed assets + current assets – current liabilities = £2,369,000 (2 marks)
   – Direct costs to company turnover = 72.04% (ie 72%) (1 mark)
   – Return on capital employed:
      £2,490,000 – £1,794,000 = £696,000 gross profit
      £696,000 – £406,000 = £ 290,000 net profit
      £290,000 as a % of £2,369,000 = 12.24%
   (2 marks)

(b) – Working capital = current assets – current liabilities:
      £204,000 – £100,000 = £104,000 (1 mark)
   – Current ratio:
      £204,000 / £100,000 = 2.04:1 (2 marks)
   – Acid-test ratio:
      £152,000 / £100,000 = 1.52:1 (2 marks)
   – The company is in a healthy position with a:
      current ratio of 2.04:1 (Ideal 2:1)
      acid-test ratio of 1.52:1 (Ideal 1:1)
   This means the company has £1.52 for every pound currently owed.
   (5 marks)

---

4. (a) Referring to the calendar extract (above), complete the spreadsheet shown below, setting out your weekly budget for fuel purchases over the next three months.

	Week 1	Week 2	Week 3	Week 4	Week 5
Month 1					
Month 2					
Month 3					

(14 marks)

OCR specimen marks:

	Week 1	Week 2	Week 3	Week 4	Week 5
Month 1	11700	17550	17550	11700	xxxxx
Month 2	17550	17550	17550	17550	xxxxx
Month 3	11700	17550	17550	17550	17550

(b) Explain the KEY factors that could affect your budget. (6 marks)

OCR specimen marks:
- allowance for fuel price increase mentioned (3 marks)
- allowance for increased business mentioned (3 marks)

5. Referring to the information on Staff in the Scenario, draw an organizational chart for Red Transport Ltd. (5 marks)

OCR specimen marks:
- Credible structure (3 marks)
- All staff covered (1 mark)
- Standard of layout (1 mark)

6. ABC Imports Ltd deals in machinery and also in dangerous goods. On checking your company records for ABC Imports Ltd, you find the only information recorded is the company name, address and telephone number. What further information would be useful to include on the records? (5 marks)

OCR specimen marks:
Any from the following list to a maximum of 5:
- Fax and/or e-mail (1 mark)
- Type of goods (1 mark)
- Volume/density/quantities/weight (1 mark)
- Dates, service used (1 mark)
- Quotes given (1 mark)
- UN classes for dangerous goods (1 mark)
- Special transport requirements (1 mark)
- Routes used (1 mark)

7. Red Transport Ltd is replacing its 2 × 4 articulated tractor units. Identify and explain the MAIN factors to be taken into account. (Consider environmental issues, compatibility with the current fleet, etc) (10 marks)

> **OCR specimen marks:**
> - Purchase price
> - Environment/noise pollution
> - Fuel economy/gear ratio/engine size
> - Wheelbase/chassis/fifth-wheel height/number of axles
> - Tax/running costs
> - Driver comfort
> - Purchase costs
>
> (5 marks for list of factors and 5 marks for valid reasons)

8. The company carries metal cages loaded with 25-litre drums of sulphuric acid on its tandem-axle box trailers. Prepare a schedule of instructions for issue to both warehouse operatives and drivers involved in this traffic. (20 marks)

> **OCR specimen marks:**
>
> Accept instructions in various formats:
> - Core
> - Warehouse operatives
> - Drivers
>
> (15 marks for actual instructions)
> - Credible structure (appropriate style)/logical sequence (2 marks)
> - Unambiguous/clarity/coherent (3 marks)

INTERNATIONAL SCENARIO

Jones International Ltd

Jones International Ltd is a young company that has been very successful in international transportation and providing logistics solutions. It has separated the company into FOUR main areas of work, each controlled by a general manager. All fleet and transport-related issues are your responsibility and you report directly to the managing director.

The most successful route you have is to Turkey via Belgium, the Netherlands, Germany, Switzerland and Italy. The company is registered in the UK for VAT purposes and has no agents abroad. The company has insurance to cover its CMR liability.

SECTION A

Read the Case-Study Scenario and answer ALL questions. You should spend approximately 30 minutes on this section of the examination.

1. A two-man crew operates on the Turkish route. What is the maximum amount of time for which they can drive the vehicle in a 30-hour period? (1 mark)

> **OCR specimen marks:**
> – 20 hours (1 mark)

2. One of your vehicles has been involved in an accident in Italy, as a result of which the 'O' licence disc is missing. What other document would your drivers have with them to indicate that the vehicle was operating on an international 'O' licence? (1 mark)

> **OCR specimen marks:**
> – Community Authorization (1 mark)

3. The route used formerly was via Yugoslavia using the TIR system. What customs transit system do you now use for the majority of the journey? (1 mark)

> **OCR specimen marks:**
> – Comunity Common Transit System (1 mark)

4. In which country on the Turkish route would you expect to have to pay vehicle tax for the vehicle to transit? (1 mark)

> **OCR specimen marks:**
> – Switzerland (1 mark)

5. Name the TWO operating companies which operate the 'piggy-back' system used in France and Germany. (2 marks)

> **OCR specimen marks:**
> – Novatrans, Kombiverkehr (2 marks)

6. What type of cargo would you normally be carrying if the vehicle was operating under the ATP Agreement? (1 mark)

> **OCR specimen marks:**
> – Perishable goods or refrigerated goods (1 mark)

7. Name the TWO international agreements that cover the movement of dangerous goods on the specified route (NB: the English Channel is being crossed by ferry)? (2 marks)

> **OCR specimen marks:**
> – ADR & IMDG (2 marks)

8. The route specified passes through certain countries that require you to obtain a Euro vignette to use their motorway networks. What would be the maximum GVW at which you could operate in order to avoid this charge? (1 mark)

> **OCR specimen marks:**
> – 12,000 kg (1 mark)

9. One of the company's vehicles has been involved in a minor accident whilst travelling under TIR. The vehicle is still roadworthy, but the impact to the vehicle caused the seals on the load compartment to break. What should the driver do with the TIR carnet in these circumstances? (1 mark)

> **OCR specimen marks:**
> – Request police or customs officer to complete the accident and note the new seal numbers in the report (1 mark)

10. Where would you obtain an ATA carnet from? (1 mark)

> **OCR specimen marks:**
> – Chamber of Commerce (1 mark)

11. Where would you obtain Eco points from? (1 mark)

OCR specimen marks:
   - International Road Freight Office (IRFO) (1 mark)

---

12. For a shipment of cargo requiring full customs formalities to be carried out, which form would you use for this? (1 mark)

OCR specimen marks:
   - SAD document or C88 (1 mark)

SECTION B

You should spend approximately 30 minutes on this section of the examination.
13. A customer has made a claim for damage to goods sent through your company to Denmark. The work was subcontracted by yourselves and subcontracted again.
   (a) What action will you take to deal with the claim? (5 marks)

OCR specimen marks:
   - Check CMR note (1 mark)
   - Notify claim to subcontractors (1 mark)
   - Notify claim to insurers (3 marks)

   (b) Explain the possible legal obligations of all involved with regard to liability? (9 marks)

OCR specimen marks:
   - Liability of successive carriers (3 marks)
   - CMR liability of first carrier (1 mark)
   - Possible defences (1 mark)
   - Limit of liability (1 mark)
   - Liability of insolvent carriers (1 mark)
   - Time limits for legal claims (3 marks)

14. The drivers on the Turkish route specified operate as a two-man crew and are out of the country for 18 days at a time. Describe the system that you would use to control their tachograph charts and explain what you would see as being the main obstacles you will need to overcome to ensure good control. (10 marks)

> **OCR specimen marks:**
> - System of control viability (5 marks)
> - Problem of chart return (2 marks)
> - Problem of cross-reference (2 marks)
> - Checking of two individual drivers' charts and comparing for that journey (1 mark)

15. You have been asked to identify the costs that you would expect the company to incur for a movement to Turkey, which are in addition to those that would be expected on a national journey. List them. (5 marks)

> **OCR specimen marks:**
> Any five from the following list, at one point each:
> - Tax at Swiss border
> - Driver subsistence
> - Ferry costs
> - Tolls
> - Euro vignette
> - Higher vehicle insurance
> - CMR insurance
> - Telephone calls

TOTAL MARKS FOR SECTION B: 29
TOTAL MARKS FOR PAPER: 43

Acknowledgement: The above text, comprising case-study scenarios, questions and specimen marks, has been reproduced by courtesy of OCR, Coventry, with thanks.

CHAPTER 14

Typical case studies and questions

The following case-study scenario and accompanying set of questions is not set out particularly to replicate the case studies and questions included in the OCR's official CPC examination. Its purpose is to encourage potential examination candidates to read a scenario and to consider all its likely implications. Just as in your real-life job, finding the right answers means determining, for example, such questions as:

- what regulations may be applicable and how these should be complied with;
- what financial considerations are relevant and how these should be calculated and budgeted for;
- what operational and technical provisions may apply;
- what licences, official forms and other documents are or may be relevant;
- where and how these documents should be obtained and completed;
- what documentation drivers should carry with them depending on the nature of their load and their destination;
- what health and safety provisions and employee legislation may apply;
- which, if any, international agreements are relevant.

Not all of these considerations will necessarily apply to the case studies presented in the official examination. However, it is quite possible that they may apply and so the candidate should get used to the idea of taking a given situation and thinking through *all* the possible requirements and implications, plus the potential hazards and shortcomings that might arise if this was a real-life scenario. Put yourself in the position of the manager charged with planning, setting-up and running the operation described – the one who carries the can if things go wrong – and focus on the key things that you would need to consider and act upon to ensure the operation runs safely, legally, efficiently, and meets customer requirements.

Note: With these questions, it's not a case of 'guess the answer', but a case of 'think up the answer'!

CASE STUDY

XYZ Trucking Ltd is a small, recently formed general haulage company based in northern England. From small beginnings the company is expanding rapidly and is constantly seeking new opportunities and new markets. It is, however, clearly committed to operating strictly within the law and in accordance with best practice and quality standards. It believes in acting professionally both towards its employees and in projecting its image to the outside world.

The firm operates a small office, a distribution warehouse and it carries out its own fleet maintenance. It currently runs 10 vehicles, comprising a mix of artics and rigids with both conventional flat-platform and curtain-sided bodies. In accordance with its professional image, the firm is seeking to ensure that its vehicles meet the highest environmental standards.

Not being content to sit back awaiting traffic that may arrive on its doorstep, the firm is actively seeking to expand its marketing activities, but at the same time without over-reaching its current secure financial base. Among the avenues being explored are the possibilities of:

- expanding its fleet by creating contracted owner–driver operators;
- developing in one or more specialist areas such as international, refrigerated and/or dangerous-goods traffics;
- developing contracted third-party logistics services;
- creating targeted 'added-value' services.

QUESTIONS

1. As part of its expansion plans, XYZ Trucking is seeking to establish a number of its senior drivers as owner–drivers, initially supported financially by the firm. It plans to supply them with a new vehicle on a hire-purchase arrangement, provide them with regular work and fund their diesel fuel purchases.

    1.1 What are the key legal considerations to take into account before this plan can be put into operation?

    1.2 What steps will need to be taken by the individual drivers to become self-employed?

    1.3 What requirements will have to be met for the drivers to secure an 'O' licence?

2. The directors of XYZ Trucking Ltd are keen to ensure that the company's health and safety standards are satisfactory.

    2.1 What key steps should they take?

    2.2 If an employee falls from the back of a vehicle while loading and breaks their leg, what steps should the firm take?

3. You are taking over as the company's fleet manager.

    3.1 What first steps would you take to ensure the law was being fully complied with?

    3.2 What would you expect to see by way of official notices on the vehicle workshop notice board?

4. You are preparing a new set of employment contracts for your employees.

    4.1 What basic information should be included?

    4.2 As a road transport employer, what additional provisions would you insert in employees' contracts of employment?

5. A new customer asks the firm to undertake a series of loads to a destination in France.

    5.1 What basic steps would need to be taken to carry out this work?

    5.2 What cross-channel alternatives would be considered in determining the best routes to the destination?

6. Following a recent visit from the enforcement officer, the firm is keen to tighten up its system for controlling tachograph charts.

    6.1 What key aspects of the charts should it be examining?

    6.2 What system of filing and retention should be employed?

7. The company decides it should upgrade its marketing efforts to raise its profile and increase sales.

    7.1 What three key steps should it take, to achieve what purpose?

    7.2 What public relations exercises might improve relations with local residents?

8. With business expanding rapidly, the directors of XYZ Trucking Ltd are trying to determine how best to handle the growth.
   8.1 State two basic alternatives they should be considering and the main pros and cons for each.

9. The company has environmental issues uppermost in mind.
   9.1 What key steps could it take to ensure its vehicles are environmentally friendly?
   9.2 What other steps could it take to improve its environmental image?

10. With its new international traffic starting to move, the company is concerned to control its additional costs effectively.
    10.1 What key elements of additional cost are likely to be incurred?
    10.2 If exchange rates between sterling and foreign currencies fluctuate during a journey, what is the effect on expenses?

11. XYZ Trucking Ltd is looking to offer 'added-value' services as part of its portfolio.
    11.1 What four such services might be considered?
    11.2 What are the pros and cons of offering added-value services?

12. In considering other avenues for expansion, the company decides to look into the possibility of setting up a dangerous-goods operation.
    12.1 What essential legal factors would need to be taken into account?
    12.2 What difficulties might the firm face in seeking to fulfil this ambition?

13. While seeking to expand its business XYZ Trucking Ltd needs to look at additional funding.
    13.1 How might this be achieved?
    13.2 What are the key pros and cons of these alternatives?

14. XYZ Trucking Ltd is thinking of buying new vehicles.
    14.1 What key specification factors would it need to take into account?
    14.2 When considering the most suitable tyres to fit to vehicles what are the key factors?

15. In response to customer requests, the company is thinking of becoming involved in intermodal transport.
    15.1 What are the key elements in an intermodal journey?
    15.2 What key items of equipment would the company need to operate intermodal services effectively?
    15.3 What are the most likely routes and destinations for intermodal consignments?

16. XYZ Trucking Ltd is preparing to operate a number of international journeys.

16.1 What key items/documents should the driver carry with them on these journeys?

16.2 Besides subsistence expenses, what other costs may the driver have to pay?

17. The company is anxious to control its vehicle operating costs.

17.1 What three key cost elements must it take into account?

17.2 What key elements of actual running costs should be recorded?

17.3 What most important overall vehicle cost should the company be looking at?

CHAPTER 15

Answers to typical case-study questions

1.1
(a) The need to change the drivers' status from PAYE employees to self-employment.
(b) The need for the drivers to become professionally competent.
(c) The need for the drivers each to obtain their own 'O' licence.

1.2
(a) Ensure they meet the Inland Revenue definition of self-employment.
(b) Notify the DSS of the change in their employment status.
(c) Set up a separate business bank account after discussing the project with their bank manager.
(d) Contact the DSS and arrange to pay self-employed National Insurance contributions (eg by direct debit).
(e) Notify the Inland Revenue that they are to become self-employed.
(f) Register for VAT (if appropriate).
(g) Decide on a name for their business if not using their own names.
(h) If trading under a name other than their own, place a notice in their premises and on their stationery showing their own name and their trading name (eg John Smith, t/a Highways Haulage).
(i) Obtain the Professional Competence qualification either by their passing the exam themselves, or getting somebody else to do so (eg an employee or wife/partner).
(j) Make sure satisfactory arrangements are made for vehicle maintenance.
(k) Apply for an 'O' licence.

1.3
They must:
(a) become professionally competent;
(b) be able to meet appropriate financial standards;
(c) be of good repute (ie not have a past record of convictions for transport offences or other serious offences);
(d) advertise their 'O' licence application;
(e) have a suitable place (ie operating centre) to park their vehicle when it is not in use;
(f) have made suitable arrangements for the maintenance of their vehicle.

2.1
(a) Define a health and safety policy and inform all the staff.
(b) Appoint a safety representative (if required).
(c) Carry out a series of risk assessments in all departments (ie office, workshop, warehouse).
(d) Assess the use of hazardous substances under COSHH regulations.
(e) Carry out a fire-risk assessment.
(f) Set up suitable first-aid facilities.
(g) Set up a system for accident reporting (as per RIDDOR).

2.2
(a) Make the employee comfortable, but do not move them.
(b) Call for an ambulance immediately.
(c) Inform the employee's family.
(d) Make an appropriate entry in the firm's accident book.
(e) Report to the Health and Safety Executive under RIDDOR.
(f) Investigate the causes of the accident.
(g) Take appropriate measure to prevent a repetition (eg by issue of instructions to staff).

3.1
(a) Obtain a copy of the firm's current vehicle fleet list.
(b) Check the fleet list against the 'O' licence to ensure all operational vehicles are authorized on the licence.
(c) Check to ensure that all vehicles have current test certificates.
(d) Check to ensure that all vehicles have had recent safety inspections.
(e) Check that wall charts show due dates for future safety inspections and annual tests.
(f) Check that all vehicle maintenance record procedures are being followed (eg driver defect reporting) and that records are up to date.
(g) Check list of company drivers and their licence details, and find out when last driving-licence inspections were carried out.
(h) Check fleet insurance details.

3.2
(a) Relevant Fire notices.
(b) Relevant Health and Safety notices.
(c) A copy of the firm's Employer's Liability Insurance certificate.
(d) A copy of the firm's Health and Safety policy.
(e) A notice about where/to whom accidents should be reported.

4.1
(a) Employer's name and address.
(b) Date when an individual's employment commenced.
(c) Job title and description.
(d) Place of work, start and finish times.
(e) Rates of pay and how and when payment of wages/salaries is made.
(f) Annual holiday and public holiday entitlements.
(g) Health examination requirements.
(h) Sick pay provisions.
(i) Grievance and disciplinary procedures.

4.2
(a) A requirement that they hold full driving licences covering the categories of vehicles operated by the company.
(b) A requirement that any contraventions of road-traffic law and driving-licence penalties are reported to the company immediately.
(c) A requirement that driving licences are produced regularly for inspection.
(d) Additional disciplinary code items to the effect that the employment may be terminated in the event of:
   • loss of driving entitlement;
   • breaches of the drivers' hours law;
   • breaches of the tachograph law;
   • any interference with the tachograph or speed limiter.

5.1
(a) Check or obtain an international 'O' licence and Community Authorizations.
(b) Check whether or not the goods to be carried are in 'free circulation' within the EU – this will determine Customs requirements.
(c) Obtain CMR liability goods-in-transit insurance cover.
(d) Obtain CMR consignment notes from the RHA.

5.2
(a) Cross-channel ferry services.
(b) The Eurotunnel freight shuttle.

6.1

(a) Whether every driver produces a completed chart for each day on which they drive a relevant vehicle.

(b) That chart centre-field details are properly completed.

(c) That driving, break and rest periods comply with the law.

(d) That any non-recorded periods of time are properly recorded on the chart manually, but without obscuring recordings or causing damage to the chart.

(e) That top speed recordings do not indicate speeding (ie above speed-limiter or the national maximum speed limits).

6.2

(a) Charts should be filed in date order and either by driver name or vehicle registration number.

(b) Charts must be retained available for inspection for at least 12 months.

7.1

(a) Advertise – to gain spread the word about the company's business activities.

(b) Set up a public relations exercise – to improve image.

(c) Undertake sales promotion – to encourage increased sales.

7.2

(a) Sending a letter to residents to explain the problems of keeping noise and pollution to a minimum.

(b) Having an 'open day' to allow residents to meet the company directors face-to-face, see what goes on in the depot and to understand the importance of the work being done.

(c) Funding local charities and events (eg in schools or local sports clubs).

8.1

(a) Increasing their own fleet – this gives them maximum control over the operation but means more capital investment and the need to employ more drivers.

(b) Subcontracting the work to small independent hauliers – this gets the work done without additional capital investment or the employment of more staff, but it means less direct control over the operation and greater risk in the event of loss-or-damage claims from customers.

9.1

(a) Update the fleet with Euro III spec vehicles.
(b) Ensure existing vehicles meet the requirements for 'Reduced Pollution' Certificates.
(c) Ensure the fuel systems of older vehicles are properly maintained and adjusted to prevent exhaust smoking.

9.2

(a) Establish a company environmental policy.
(b) Set up systems for the proper disposal of waste.
(c) Take steps to reduce noise emanating from the premises.
(d) Provide seminars/training for all staff in understanding 'green' issues.

10.1

(a) Ferry/Eurotunnel fares.
(b) Currency exchange gains/losses.
(c) Insurance premiums, eg CMR cover.
(d) Driver expenses.
(e) Driver personal insurance cover (ie medical and personal effects)
(f) Road/bridge/tunnel tolls.
(g) Agent's commissions.
(h) Vehicle-recovery-service premiums.
(i) Communications and documentation costs.

10.2

(a) If the value of sterling falls, expenses will be greater (ie less foreign currency will be obtainable for each one pound sterling).
(b) If the value of sterling rises, expenses will be reduced (ie a greater amount of foreign currency will be obtainable for each one pound sterling).

11.1

(a) Full logistics services (eg storage, order processing, order picking and delivery on behalf of customers).
(b) Specialist packing of goods (eg for overseas shipment).
(c) Collection and redelivery of goods in connection with warranty repairs (eg domestic appliances).
(d) Installation and commissioning of engineering or electronic equipment.

11.2

(a) Makes for closer ties with the customer and the possibility of longer-term contracts.
(b) Provides extra lines of revenue.

(c) Provides for more efficient use of premises/buildings/existing staff.
(d) Requires additional initial capital investment and more staff.
(e) Requires extra staff training.
(f) Possible lack among personnel of expertise or management experience in the new business.

12.1

(a) The need to use vehicles meeting dangerous goods/ADR technical specifications (eg firescreen protection, etc).
(b) The need to employ dangerous goods/ADR trained and certified drivers.
(c) The need for a certified Dangerous Goods Safety Adviser.
(d) The need for vehicles to be labelled in accordance with UK/ADR requirements and drivers to carry TREMCARDS.

12.2

(a) Marketing their currently non-existent services to manufacturers.
(b) Convincing potential customers that they have the knowledge and experience to provide a safe and reliable haulage service.
(c) The risk of making an investment that may not lead to a successful business.

13.1

(a) By seeking outside investors to put money into the business.
(b) By finding a venture capital company to invest.
(c) By the issue of debentures or loan stock.
(d) By bank loans.
(e) By financing vehicle acquisitions with hire purchase or leasing.

13.2

(a) To seek outside investors in the form of sleeping partners or by selling equity in a private company to people known to the owners, or by floating the business on the stock exchange.
(b) A venture capital company would want to take a large shareholding and appoint their director/s to the board.
(c) Debentures are a good source of additional funds but in the event of the business collapsing debenture holders have priority over other creditors and shareholders.
(d) Bank loans leave the company under the control of its directors and shareholders, but incur high interest charges and may require personal guarantees by the directors or a charge on the business assets.
(e) Funding vehicles by hire-purchase means even higher interest charges, but a quick exit if things turn bad, albeit at a cost.

14.1

(a) Nature of loads – parcels/heavy freight/bulk liquids/granular/refrigerated.
(b) Weight/volume of loads.
(c) Nature of operation – local delivery/long-haul/international.
(d) Rigid/articulated vehicle/lorry and trailer combination (ie road train).
(e) Number of axles.
(f) Engine power/transmission.
(g) Day/sleeper cab.
(h) Special equipment (refrigeration/lorry-mounted crane/tail-lift).

14.2

(a) Size/weight rating
(b) Type – drive/steer/trailing axle.
(c) Tractive grip (traction)
(d) Directional stability
(e) Built-in kerbing protection (for local delivery vans).
(f) Potential life (miles/kilometres)
(g) Price/cost per mile.

15.1

(a) A road leg at each end of the journey.
(b) A terminal transfer at each end of the journey.
(c) A rail or inland waterway long-haul middle leg of the journey.

15.2

(a) Vehicles/trailers with skeletal or platform bodies with built-in twist-locks.
(b) ISO box/frame/bulk liquid containers.
(c) Swap bodies.
(d) Vehicles plated for 44-tonne operation (for railhead operations).
(e) A heavy-duty fork-lift truck capable of lifting containers/swap bodies.

15.3

(a) Long-haul destinations within the UK (eg southern England to Scotland).
(b) Destinations in Europe via the Channel Tunnel (eg via the Freight Shuttle).

16.1
(a) His passport and a visa where necessary.
(b) His driving licence and/or IDP (where necessary).
(c) The vehicle registration document (the original, not a copy).
(d) A letter of authority to be in charge of the vehicle.
(e) Evidence of insurance (eg a Green Card).
(f) A Community Authorization.
(g) Load documents (eg CMR consignment note/Customs documents).
(h) Road haulage permits/transit documents (eg for Austria – only where necessary depending on the route/destination.
(i) ADR/ATP certificate where appropriate.
(j) Fuel/breakdown service card.
(k) Warning triangle.
(l) Wheel chocks/fire extinguisher/spare bulbs (as appropriate).

16.2
(a) Road/bridge/tunnel tolls.
(b) On-the-spot fines.

17.1
(a) Standing/fixed costs.
(b) Running/variable costs.
(c) Establishment/overhead costs.

17.2
(a) Fuel.
(b) Drivers' wages.
(c) Tyres.
(d) Maintenance and repairs.

17.3
(a) Total life cost.

Other books by the author:

The Dangerous Goods Safety Manual: A study guide for DGSAs, 2000

The Dictionary of Transport and Logistics: Contains over 3,000 terms and abbreviations, 2002

The Pocket Guide to LGV Drivers' Hours & Tachograph Law, 2nd edn, 2004

The Professional LGV Driver's Handbook, 2nd edn, 2004

A Study Manual of Professional Competence in Road Haulage, 11th edn, 2004

Transport Manager's and Operator's Handbook 2005, 35th edn, 2005

The above titles are available from all good bookshops or direct from the publishers. To obtain more information, please contact the publishers at the address below:

Kogan Page
120 Pentonville Road
London N1 9JN
Tel: 020 7278 0433
Fax: 020 7837 6348
www.kogan-page.co.uk